FINISHING
STRONG

FINISHING STRONG

HOW A MAN CAN GO THE DISTANCE

STEVE FARRAR

MULTNOMAH BOOKS
SISTERS, OREGON

FINISHING STRONG
published by Multnomah Books
a part of the Questar publishing family

© 1995 by Steve Farrar
International Standard Book Number: 1-57673-023-9

Cover design by David Carlson

Cover illustration by Michael Schwab

Edited by Larry Libby

Printed in the United States of America

Most Scripture quotations are from:
New American Standard Bible (NASB)
© 1960, 1977 by the Lockman Foundation

Also quoted:
The Holy Bible, New International Version (NIV)
© 1973, 1984 by International Bible Society,
used by permission of Zondervan Publishing House

The Living Bible (TLB)
© 1971 by Tyndale House Publishers

Please note: Chapter Eight appeared in *If I'm Not Tarzan, and My Wife Isn't Jane,
Then What Are We Doing in the Jungle?* an earlier, now out-of-print book by the author.

For information:
QUESTAR PUBLISHERS, INC.
POST OFFICE BOX 1720
SISTERS, OREGON 97759

97 98 99 00 01 02 — 10 9 8 7 6 5 4 3 2

To my brothers,

Mike Farrar
and
Jeff Farrar

We have been running this race together now for over forty years.

When one has tripped, there have been two to pick him up.

And that's the best part of this race.

We're running in it together.

We were given a great start.

Let's have a strong finish.

Together.

Thank you for your encouragement.

It's great to have brothers who are brothers.

CONTENTS

Basketball, football, and baseball are team sports—and so is writing a book. And there are some valuable members of this team who should be specifically put into the spotlight.

Simply put, Larry Libby is a superb editor. This is our third project together, and once again, Larry showed his stuff. Thanks, Larry, for your tireless work and ceaseless encouragement.

Thanks also to David Kopp, who provided some *very* timely direction and focus! Way to go, Dave!

My brother-in-law, Bryan Owens, did a great job of overseeing the ministry side of things so that I could channel my energies into this book.

Thanks to Dr. Howard Hendricks for his willingness to plug in some significant data that enabled me to shape the central premise of this book. And I am indebted to Dr. Robert Clinton for taking the time in several phone conversations to summarize his substantial studies of over nine hundred Christian leaders.

Dr. Charlie Dyer, professor of Old Testament at Dallas Theological Seminary, also lent his biblical expertise on more than one occasion. Thanks, Charlie! I'll buy you a Diet Dr. Pepper in Jerusalem when we make that Israel trip!

Dave Roper introduced me to Manasseh and Uzziah a long time ago at Peninsula Bible Church. Much of what I have written is gleaned from Dave's great studies of twenty-five years ago.

Jim Litchfield, Mario Zandstra, Ken Sibley, Pat Hamner, Mike Farrar, and John Bethany all took their valuable time to read assorted drafts and offer critical input. Thanks, gentlemen!

My in-laws, Carl and Sara Jo Wilson, made some significant personal sacrifices out of their own schedules to help make this book a reality, and I am grateful to them.

At our house, writing a book is always a family effort. Mary, Rachel, John, and Josh all made significant personal sacrifices to enable me to write. Especially toward the end of the project when I got irritable because I was trying to finish strong! Thanks for putting up with me. You are the four earthly reasons *why* I want to finish strong.

PART ONE

THE PRIORITY OF
FINISHING STRONG

ONE OUT
OF TEN

———————◁

Truth is heavy, so few men carry it.

JEWISH PROVERB

The year 1994 was a great year for the NBA draft.

Three players emerged from the '94 draft who were destined for greatness: Grant Hill, Jason Kidd, and Glenn Robinson. It's a rare year when there are *three* young players available who single-handedly can turn a franchise around. But '94 was one of those years.

Hill impacted Detroit, Kidd revolutionized the Dallas Mavericks, and Robinson made Milwaukee a potential threat to every team in the league. And when it came time to give the Rookie of the Year award, for only the third time in NBA history the voting was tied. As a result, Jason Kidd and Grant Hill were named Co-Rookies of the Year. And Robinson was right behind them in the balloting, breathing down their necks.

The year 1945 was remarkable, too.

As 1994 was a great year for rookie hoop stars, so 1945 was an absolutely unbelievable year for rookie evangelists. In that year, twenty-seven-year-old Billy Graham came storming out of seemingly nowhere to fill auditoriums across

America, speaking to as many as thirty thousand people a night. Graham was hired as the first full-time evangelist for Youth for Christ, and his reputation as a uniquely gifted preacher roared across America like a prairie fire. The rest, of course, is history.

You've heard of Billy Graham. But what about Chuck Templeton or Bron Clifford? Have you ever heard of them?

Billy Graham wasn't the only young preacher packing auditoriums in 1945. Chuck Templeton and Bron Clifford were accomplishing the same thing—and more. All three young men were in their midtwenties. One seminary president, after hearing Chuck Templeton preach one evening to an audience of thousands, called him "the most gifted and talented young man in America today for preaching."[1]

Templeton and Graham were friends. Both ministered for Youth for Christ. Both were extraordinary preachers. Yet in those early years, "most observers would probably have put their money on Templeton."[2] As a matter of fact, in 1946, the National Association of Evangelicals published an article on men who were "best used of God" in that organization's five-year existence. The article highlighted the ministry of Chuck Templeton. Billy Graham was never mentioned.[3] Templeton, many felt, would be the next Babe Ruth of evangelism.

Bron Clifford was yet another gifted, twenty-five-year-old fireball. In 1945, many believed Clifford the most gifted and powerful preacher the church had seen in centuries. In that same year, Clifford preached to an auditorium of thousands in Miami, Florida. People lined up ten and twelve deep outside the auditorium trying to get in. Later that same year, when Clifford was preaching in the chapel at Baylor University, the president ordered class bells turned off so that the young man could minister without interruption to the student body. For two hours and fifteen minutes, he kept those students on the edge of their seats as he preached on the subject, "Christ and the Philosopher's Stone."

> At the age of twenty-five young Clifford touched more lives, influenced
> more leaders, and set more attendance records than any other

clergyman his age in American history. National leaders vied for his attention. He was tall, handsome, intelligent, and eloquent. Hollywood invited him to audition for the part of Marcellus in "The Robe." It seemed as if he had everything.[4]

Graham, Templeton, and Clifford.

In 1945, all three came shooting out of the starting blocks like rockets. You've heard of Billy Graham. So how come you've never heard of Chuck Templeton or Bron Clifford? Especially when they came out of the chutes so strong in '45.

Just five years later, Templeton left the ministry to pursue a career as a radio and television commentator and newspaper columnist. Templeton had decided he was no longer a believer in Christ in the orthodox sense of the term. By 1950, this future Babe Ruth wasn't even in the game and no longer believed in the validity of the claims of Jesus Christ.

What about Clifford? By 1954, Clifford had lost his family, his ministry, his health, and then…his life. Alcohol and financial irresponsibility had done him in. He wound up leaving his wife and their two Down's syndrome children. At just thirty-five years of age, this once great preacher died from cirrhosis of the liver in a run-down motel on the edge of Amarillo. His last job was selling used cars in the panhandle of Texas. He died, as John Haggai put it, "unwept, un-honored, and unsung." Some pastors in Amarillo took up a collection among themselves in order to purchase a casket so that his body could be shipped back East for decent burial in a cemetery for the poor.

In 1945, three young men with extraordinary gifts were preaching the gospel to multiplied thousands across this nation. Within ten years, only one of them was still on track for Christ.

In the Christian life, it's not how you start that matters. It's how you finish.

John Bisagno has been pastoring First Baptist of Houston for a number of years. When John was just about to finish college, he was having dinner over at his fiancée's house one night. After supper, he was talking with his future father-in-law, Dr. Paul Beck, out on the porch. Dr. Beck had been in ministry for years, and that was inevitably the subject toward which the conversation turned.

"John, as you get ready to enter the ministry, I want to give you some advice," Dr. Beck told the younger man. "Stay true to Jesus! Make sure that you keep your heart close to Jesus every day. It's a long way from here to where you're going to go, and Satan's in no hurry to get you."

The older man continued. "It has been my observation that just one out of ten who start out in full-time service for the Lord at twenty-one are still on track by the age of sixty-five. They're shot down morally, they're shot down with discouragement, they're shot down with liberal theology, they get obsessed with making money…but for one reason or another nine out of ten fall out."

The twenty-year-old Bisagno was shocked.

"I just can't believe that!" he said. "That's impossible! That just can't be true."

Bisagno told how he went home, took one of those blank pages in the back of his Scofield Reference Bible and wrote down the names of twenty-four young men who were his peers and contemporaries. These were young men in their twenties who were sold out for Jesus Christ. They were trained for ministry and burning in their desire to be used by the Lord. These were the committed young preachers who would make an impact for the Lord in their generation.

Bisagno relates the following with a sigh: "I am now fifty-three years old. From time to time as the years have gone by, I've had to turn back to that page in my Bible and cross out a name. I wrote down those twenty-four names when I was just twenty years of age. Thirty-three years later, there are only *three names* remaining of the original twenty-four."

In the Christian life, it's not how you start that matters. It's how you finish.

Preaching several years ago in Scotland, John MacArthur Jr. was approached by a man after the service.

"Is your father named Jack MacArthur?" the man asked.

MacArthur said yes.

"Your father came to Ireland over thirty years ago with two other men to hold a revival in Belfast and in other parts of the country. I went to hear your father speak, and at that meeting I received Jesus Christ and dedicated my life to the ministry. I am a pastor because the Lord used your father to minister to me. Would you tell him that when you see him?"

MacArthur indicated that he would, and then the man asked another question.

"Where is your father now?"

MacArthur told him that his father was preaching and pastoring.

The man then asked, "Is he still faithful to the Word?"

"Yes, he is still faithful and still standing."

"What happened to the other two men who were ministering with your father?"

MacArthur replied, "I'm sorry to report that one has denied the faith and the other died an alcoholic."[5]

There it is again. Three relatively young men, completely committed to Christ, make their way to Ireland to preach the gospel. They see God do great things. But thirty years later when the dust had settled, only one out of the three was still standing.

In the Christian life, it's not how you start that matters. It's how you finish.

Graham made it; Templeton and Clifford didn't. Bisagno and two of his buddies are all that's left out of twenty-four young men who thirty-some years ago were ready to die, if necessary, for Jesus Christ. Jack MacArthur and his two friends were greatly used by God. But thirty years later only Jack is standing strong.

Are these stories exceptions to the rule? I only wish they were.

Dr. Howard Hendricks recently conducted a study of 246 men in full-time ministry who experienced personal moral failure within a two-year period. In other words, Hendricks was able to find nearly 250 men who derailed within twenty-four months of each other. That's roughly ten a month for two years. Ten guys a month in moral failure. That's two, almost three, guys a week. And each of them started strong.

In the Christian life, it's not how you start that matters. It's how you finish.

You may be thinking, "Those are interesting stories, but they really don't relate to me. I'm not in full-time ministry." I'm sorry to rock your boat, but if you are a Christian, and if you are serious about following Christ, then you surely are in the ministry. Full-time. Are you a husband? Do you have kids? If the answer is yes, then you're implicated! Christian husbands and fathers *are* in the ministry full-time. *The enemy just doesn't want you to realize it.*

You may not collect your paycheck from a church each week, but according to Ephesians 4:11–13 and Colossians 3:23, that's not the issue. I don't care if you're a truck driver, a CEO, or a golf pro. Whatever your profession, if you know Jesus Christ as your Lord and Savior, then ultimately you work for Him.

Jesus said that *you* are the light of the world. Jesus said that *you* are the salt of the earth. And He didn't mention anything about "part-time."

John Bisagno's father-in-law stated that from his experience only one out of ten men who start strong in their twenties will still be on track with Christ at sixty-five. Now here's my question to you, and I want you to think about it carefully.

What makes you think that you will be the one man out of ten who finishes strong?

What makes you think that you won't be one of the nine who fall short of the mark? The man who finishes strong, after all, is the exception. Why? Because *when it comes to finishing strong, the odds are against you.* Finishing strong is not impossible. It is, however, improbable. It's going to take some tough choices and an experience or two of personal brokenness in order to have a strong finishing kick when you hit the tape at age sixty-five, seventy-five, eighty-five, or whenever it is that God calls you home.

- It is the rare man who finishes strong.

- It is the exceptional man who finishes strong.

- It is the teachable man who finishes strong.

So here's the question. What *exceptional measures* are you taking in your life to ensure that you will be the one out of ten?

John Maxwell tells the story of the scout who called up Charlie Grimm when he was managing the Chicago Cubs. The scout was so enthusiastic he could hardly get the words out.

"Charlie! I've just come across the greatest young pitcher I have ever seen! He struck out every man who came to bat. Twenty-seven came up and twenty-seven struck out! Nobody even hit a foul ball until the ninth inning. I've got the kid right here with me. Do you want me to sign him?"

"No," replied Charlie. "Find the guy who hit the foul ball and sign *him*. I'm looking for hitters." Charlie knew what he was looking for, and he didn't waver.

Charlie wasn't looking for pitchers, he was looking for hitters. There are a lot of guys who have started in the Christian life, but God is looking for some *finishers*. That's what this book is about. It's about finishing. Finishing strong. It's about being the one out of ten. But the chances are that you won't be. If you stay on cruise control, my friend, you can count on being in the nine out of ten rather than the one out of ten.

Maybe someone is reading this and musing to himself, "Those are some thought-provoking illustrations, but what is your scriptural basis for 'one-out-of-ten'? Is there a specific verse that teaches that principle?"

No, there isn't a specific verse. But as we observe life and the fact that so many who start out strong in the Christian life get derailed by one thing or another, that "one out of ten" number seems right in the ballpark. Maybe I can't prove one out of ten directly from the Scriptures.

But how about two out of twelve?

> Then the LORD spoke to Moses saying, "Send out for yourself men so
> that they may spy out the land of Canaan, which I am going to give to
> the sons of Israel; you shall send a man from each of their fathers' tribes,
> every one a *leader* among them." (Numbers 13:1–2)

You know the story. God is ready to hand over the keys to the Promised Land to the newly liberated nation of Israel. Under the leadership of Moses, He has brought them out of Egypt after four hundred years of slavery. The two million plus people left Egypt with the gold and riches of Egypt in their possession. And now they are poised to enter the rich and prosperous land that will be their new home.

God specifically instructs Moses to pick out twelve men, one from each tribe. But He is even more specific than that. He tells him to pick twelve *leaders*. And that's what Moses did. He picked men from each tribe who had already proven themselves as leaders—Israel's best and brightest. They weren't rookies; they were salty veterans. These were the men with proven track records and vision for the future. Let's put it this way: Moses wasn't going to pick wannabees or has-beens to go check out the land. For a mission like that you don't send the third string—you send in your starters. Your main men. Twelve of them to be specific.

And out of those twelve, only two finished strong.

You may question the one out of ten, but if you take the Scriptures seriously, there is no questioning the two out of twelve. Israel waited for forty years to enter the land because ten guys who had started strong—ten guys who had seen God send the plagues to Egypt...ten guys who had seen God open the Red Sea for them and their families, and then close it on Pharaoh's army...ten guys who had seen God work time and time again on their behalf—freaked out because the land contained some very powerful tribes and fortified cities. In other words, the ten had a greater fear of man than they did of God. And this was after all the mind-boggling miracles God had performed before their very eyes! It was E. Stanley Jones who said, "Fear is the sand in the machinery of life." And it brought these ten leaders to a lurching, staggering halt.

These ten leaders had a great start. They just couldn't finish. And they delayed Israel's realization of the Promised Land for forty weary years. A whole generation perished in the bleak sands of the Sinai because these guys got sand in their gears.

This book is about being a Joshua and a Caleb—and not being a Shammua, Shaphat, Igal, Palti, Gaddiel, Gaddi, Ammiel, Sethur, Nahbi, or Geuel. These were names of the twelve spies. Of the original twelve, ten derailed. Only Joshua and Caleb had taken the time to develop their moral and spiritual character so that they had the faith and endurance to trust in God when the chips were down. We still name our boys Joshua today, don't we? And we name them Caleb. (My son, Joshua, is even now swimming on this hot July afternoon with his friend from down the street—Caleb.) But I don't know of any couples who want to name their sons Shaphat or Palti. Those are names that have been forgotten—and so have the men who wore them.

There must have been some very good reasons why these ten men were chosen to scope out the Promised Land. At least there were some good external reasons. The problem is, no one but God can look into a man's heart.

You can bet that each of these ten guys, if he were around today, would be at church faithfully every Sunday morning and Sunday night. He'd be there for Wednesday night fellowship dinner. He'd show up on Tuesday for choir practice and teach Sunday school. He would be a tither and serve on the board. Externally, all of these guys looked like dynamite. But when push came to shove, only two out of ten had what it took. And the difference was all on the inside.

You see, it's *endurance* that separates the men from the boys. It's *endurance* that determines whether or not a man will finish strong. And endurance is the fruit of godly character. The Christian life isn't a hundred-yard dash. It's a marathon. It's a long race, and long races don't require speed. They require grit, determination, and finishing power.

As Scripture says:

> Therefore, since we have so great a cloud of witnesses surrounding us,
> let us also lay aside every encumbrance, and the sin which so easily
> entangles us, and let us run with endurance the race that is set before
> us, fixing our eyes on Jesus. (Hebrews 12:1–2)

You may be reading this and thinking that it's too late for you to finish strong. You've made some mistakes. Some big mistakes. You may think you could *never* finish strong because:

- you've been through a divorce—and it was pretty much your fault;
- you got involved in a sexual affair and violated your vows to your wife and to your God;
- you've made some very serious ethical and moral choices that have caused you to lose credibility with your family, friends, and associates.

Listen, my friend, it's never too late to begin doing what's right. As long as you're breathing, it's never too late to confess your sin to the Lord in genuine repentance and receive His forgiveness. You may have messed up and messed up big-time, but unless I miss my guess, you're still probably a long way from the finish line. Thanks to the grace of God, you've got time to make up a lot of ground. Just because you've fallen down doesn't mean that you can't get up and finish strong.

I've never been big on poems, but here and there I bump into an exception. Here's a good one that is also long. And that's why I'm going to cut out the opening verses and go right to the last several stanzas. All you need to know to pick it up is that it's the story of a young boy competing in a race he desperately wants to win. But he has fallen down three times. And each time his dad has urged him to get up and win the race. Read these lines slowly. That way you'll get not only the meat, but also the juices.

THE RACE

Defeat! He lay there silently, a tear dropped from his eye.
"There's no sense running anymore—three strikes, I'm out—why try?"
The will to rise had disappeared, all hope had fled away,
So far behind, so error prone, closer all the way.
"I've lost, so what's the use," he thought, "I'll live with my disgrace."
But then he thought about his dad who soon he'd have to face.
"Get up," an echo sounded low, "Get up and take your place.
You were not meant for failure here, so get up and win the race."

With borrowed will, "Get up," it said, "You haven't lost at all,

For winning is not more than this—to rise each time you fall."

So up he rose to win once more, and with a new commit,

He resolved that win or lose, at least he wouldn't quit.

So far behind the others now, the most he'd ever been,

Still he gave it all he had and ran as though to win.

Three times he'd fallen stumbling, three times he rose again,

Too far behind to hope to win, he still ran to the end.

They cheered the winning runner as he crossed, first place,

Head high and proud and happy; no falling, no disgrace.

But when the fallen youngster crossed the line, last place,

The crowd gave him the greater cheer for finishing the race.

And even though he came in last, with head bowed low, unproud;

You would have thought he won the race, to listen to the crowd.

And to his dad he sadly said, "I didn't do so well."

"To me, you won," his father said. "You rose each time you fell."

And now when things seem dark and hard and difficult to face,

The memory of that little boy helps me in my race.

For all of life is like that race, with ups and downs and all,

And all you have to do to win—is rise each time you fall.

"Quit! Give up, you're beaten," they still shout in my face.

But another voice within me says, "Get up and win that race."

—AUTHOR UNKNOWN

When I read this poem, I think of the story of David Flood. Flood was a Swede who committed his life to Jesus Christ in his youth. He married a young woman named Svea who shared his commitment to Christ. They felt called to serve the Lord in Africa and arrived on those distant shores in 1921. With all their hearts, they wanted to work among people who had never heard the gospel. As it turned out, the work was hard, the conditions horrible, and the people hostile and unresponsive. Their lives were constantly in danger.

The Floods had two children in those conditions. Shortly after the second child was born, Svea died. David, already consumed by doubts and discouraged by a lack of results, was devastated. All he had to show for his efforts was just one convert...one young boy. He had sacrificed his wife and the best years of his life. For what? For *one* kid?

He had been a fool for bringing Svea to this hostile and cruel situation. He was eaten by guilt and despair. And it was under that cloud of defeat and failure that he decided to leave Africa. He took his young son with him, yet had to leave his infant daughter behind since she was too ill to travel.

A missionary couple took her in and when they subsequently died, she was passed on to another missionary couple, who later raised her in America. In the meantime, David, who was living in Sweden, turned his back on the faith. After his second marriage dissolved, he began living with a mistress. He thought little of the daughter whom he had not seen since infancy.

His daughter, Aggie, however, thought about him often. She had learned about the work he and her mother had begun in Africa, and she desperately wanted to talk with him about it. Aggie later married and together with her husband lived in America. But with all her heart she wanted to find her father.

Years later she was able to arrange the trip to Sweden. She found her seventy-three-year-old, bedridden father living in a shabby apartment littered with liquor bottles. She went to her father and told him she still loved him...and that God did, too.

And then she told him about his one convert.

That little boy had grown up to be a gifted leader and minister of the gospel. That one little boy eventually led thousands of others to Christ and helped to establish the church of Jesus Christ in that section of Africa. Upon hearing what God had done, David threw himself on the mercy of God. He asked God to forgive his rebellion and wasted years. And God did. David didn't know that he had just six months to live. But those six months were months of productivity and restoring broken relationships.

After nearly forty years of falling on his face, David Flood got up and finished the race. And believe it or not, he actually finished strong.[6]

If the Lord can do that for someone like David Flood, then He can do it for you. It's never too late to get back on course and pursue Christ with your whole heart.

Finishing strong does not mean finishing unblemished.

Finishing strong does not mean finishing perfect.

That is impossible.

> Standards of life-style and conduct for those in the Christian ministry
> are rooted in the Old Testament patriarchs, leaders, and prophets.
> They were approved by God for the way they lived. That did not mean
> they were perfect. The Bible is absolutely honest about their sins and
> failure. It records these, sometimes in embarrassing detail, so that we
> may learn from them and avoid their failures (Romans 15:4).[7]

Many of those lives recorded in Scripture contain some surprises. As a matter of fact

- some who finished strong were previously involved in sexual immorality;

- some who finished strong waited until late in life to surrender to their Creator and Savior;

- some who finished strong were considered at mid-life to be utter failures;

- some who finished strong found themselves stuck in bitter circumstances, frustrated, and disappointed by situations not of their own making;

- some who finished strong overcame personal failure and major setbacks by embracing the grace of God.

If you're interested in being one of the guys who finishes strong—*no matter what your past*—then I can make you a promise. This book will help you to understand the process that God must take you through. Trust me. It is a tough course. But it is well worth the effort. God has been taking His men through this training for thousands of years. There will be days when it gets so tough you may wonder if God has abandoned you. There will certainly be days when you will seriously question if He really loves you.

But there will be other days when you will experience the favor and blessing of God beyond anything that you could ask or think. There will be days when His grace will genuinely overwhelm you and you will wonder if you can take any more of His blessing without bursting at the seams.

Finishing strong is tough. It's not for everyone because it's not easy. I admit to you that it is hard. But there is another way that is much harder. The Scriptures say that "the way of the transgressor is hard."

If you are interested in what Eugene Peterson calls "a long obedience in the same direction," then read on.

If you are interested in being the one out of ten, then read on.

If you are interested in being the man who is the exception to the rule, then read on.

Quite frankly, if you've gotten this far and you're still reading, then you *are* the exception. Too many guys are willing to do just enough to get by. Too many guys are ready to bail out of the race at the first twinge of sideache.

- Is your marriage on rough water right now? Don't quit.

- Is that secretary who is craving more of your attention starting to look more and more attractive? Don't even think about it.

- Have you gone so long without apparently seeing God say yes to one of your prayers that you're about ready to chuck this Christian thing? That would be a serious mistake.

The enemy would like to sucker us into thinking that the "easy" way is the best way. But it never is.

I have been giving a tremendous amount of thought to this chapter and its content. The other day I went to the grocery store for Mary. I was so preoccupied with this chapter that before I realized it I had driven a mile and a half beyond the store. When I finally got into the store, I couldn't remember what I was supposed to get. And then when I went out to parking lot, I couldn't remember where I'd parked my car.

Not only have I been preoccupied, but my good friend and editor, Larry Libby, has also been preoccupied with this book. We've both been preoccupied because we have seen so many guys who have made serious errors in judgment. We've had Christian friends who have left their wives and kids for another woman, and we have seen the destruction that such choices always bring.

Larry and I have been talking on the phone about the best way to get this material across. A couple of days ago my fax machine started spitting out a letter from Larry. His letter was a follow-up to our last phone conversation. And in that fax Larry had some things to say about this chapter. They were so good that I decided to let you in on Larry's wisdom.

> Steve, as I reviewed your March 23 epistle, I am encouraged. I could almost believe that these delays in the book have been divinely orchestrated to help us achieve the strongest possible message. You, Dave Kopp [senior editor], and I are all guys in our forties who recognize the sober truth of these issues. What issue in life could be more important?
>
> In regard to chapter one, I think it's the perfect way to begin. There's a scare in this chapter. A punch in the stomach. But there is also a challenge—and I think most men love a challenge. Will I be the one in ten? How can I make sure that I'm the one in ten?
>
> My only caution: Don't paint it in terms of some he-man effort in the flesh, because we all know that won't cut it. Strong men fall. Weak men who find their strength in Another don't fall. We won't be the one-in-ten because of our own strength or wisdom or courage or

perseverance or any other human quality. If we finish strong, it will only be because we have tapped into Ultimate Strength, Limitless Wisdom, the Fount of Courage, the Source of Perseverance. HE will get us across the finish line. The very gates of hell cannot make us stumble unless we choose to remove ourselves from His protection and power. I'd like to see a little hope and encouragement here that we can indeed be one of the one in ten guys who finish strong. And that's because "His divine power has given us everything we need for life and godliness."

When I read Larry's comments, I thought to myself, "He nailed it. I can't put it any better than that." Larry pretty much summed it up. Did you catch his one sentence—*"The very gates of hell cannot make us stumble unless we choose to remove ourselves from His protection and power"*? That is a significant insight.

Men who don't hit the finish line strong have *chosen* to remove themselves from the Lord's protection and power. This book is an attempt to help us understand the steps we can take to stay under His protection and power. And if we do that, guys, by His grace we're going to hit that tape and hit it hard.

By the way, where is that finish line? Well, it's different for each one of us. The finish line that I have in mind is when we go to be with the Lord. You might have forty years before you die, or you might have six months. That's the interesting thing about this race. No one knows where the finish line is. And that makes this race just that much tougher.

Runners will tell you that they want to know where the finish line is. It doesn't matter if they're running one hundred yards or a marathon, they must know where the finish line is. And when they get that finish line in sight, they block out everything else and concentrate fully and completely on the tape. That concentration on the finish, that keeping their eye on the mark, that's what enables them to blot out the pain and exhaustion and finish strong.

Not every competition allows the competitors to actually see the finish line. A friend of mine used to row in the Oxford crew. You've seen those long, sleek, beautiful shells, filled with sweating and straining men, whose movements are so amazingly synchronized as they pull those longs oars through the water.

Those men have their *backs* to the finish line! So how can they possibly finish strong? How do they pace themselves and how do they know when to sprint? If they can't see the finish line and focus upon it, then how in the world can they row an effective race? The answer is that they focus on the coxswain. He's the guy with the megaphone sitting at the end of the boat facing the crew. He's the only one who knows where the finish line is. So the men at the oars look to him, listen to him, obey his commands, and count on him to coach them to the finish. He paces them, he encourages them, and they trust him implicitly to get them across the finish line in the strongest possible way. They are counting on the coxswain to enable them to finish strong.

That's the Christian life, guys. How do we finish strong? We don't finish strong by focusing on the finish line because we don't know where the finish line is.

We finish strong by fixing our eyes on Jesus.

That's what the twelve guys who hung around with Jesus did. They were known as the disciples. And they had a much better success ratio than the guys that went into the Promised Land. Out of the first twelve, only Joshua and Caleb finished strong. But when we look at the latter twelve, all of them finished strong...with one notable exception. And why didn't he finish strong? He never did submit his life to Christ. He didn't have his eyes on Jesus—he had his eyes on the money. But the other eleven guys kept their eyes on Jesus.

No, they weren't perfect. In fact, they all fell away from the Lord for a brief time. And that was a major failure. But as Elbert Hubbard observed, "A failure is a person who has blundered but not been able to cash in on the experience." The disciples blundered, but they also cashed in on the experience...and got back on track. And even through the crucible of incredible persecution and hardship, every single one of them finished strong. And just as they finished strong, so we can finish strong. They were in the boat with Jesus, and now we are in the boat with Jesus.

In this boat, Jesus is the coxswain. And each of us is rowing. We're rowing daily and we're rowing diligently. And as we fix our gaze upon Him, He will pace us, He will encourage us, and He will instruct us. And then one day—in an instant—the race will be over! We'll cross the finish line, and life on earth will be over. And because we have listened to Him, because we have obeyed Him, we will realize that we didn't just finish.

We finished *strong*.

CHAPTER TWO

FINISHING SO-SO

—————●

Beware of no man more than yourself;
we carry our worst enemies within us.

CHARLES HADDON SPURGEON

A dog walked into a Dodge City saloon and ordered a root beer.

The barkeep snickered, "We don't serve dogs or root beer in this saloon."

The dog said, "I've got money and my money is as good as any man's. Give me a root beer!"

The bartender was tired of talking so he reached under the bar, pulled out a gun, and shot the dog in the foot. "Now get out of here and don't ever come back."

A week later, the dog came back, this time wearing his gun belt that holstered two guns. Not seeing the man who shot him behind the bar, he walked up to the new bartender, looked him squarely in the eye, and said very slowly and very deliberately, "I'm lookin' for the man who shot my paw."

John Wesley Powell has been pretty much forgotten. It used to be that every grade school kid in America knew about Powell and his amazing courage to survive a journey against all odds. As a matter of fact, a lot of people thought that Powell was nuts. The expedition was simply too dangerous.

Especially for a man with just one arm.

Why did Powell have just one arm? During the Civil War, an enemy soldier shot his paw. To be more specific, his forearm. Eventually the arm had to be amputated. But Powell never let his injury stop him from becoming a national hero.

Back in 1869 conventional wisdom said that passage through the Grand Canyon on the Colorado River was impossible. It couldn't be done. The back country surrounding the Grand Canyon oozed with legends of doomed expeditions. No one had *ever* dared that stretch of river and come out alive. Out of all the expeditions that had given it their best shot, there was not one survivor.

One army lieutenant who had explored the Colorado just on the southern side of the Grand Canyon believed that powerful river so treacherous that "the Colorado, along the greater part of its lonely and majestic way, shall be *forever unvisited* and undisturbed."[1] Did you see the movie *The River Wild*? If you did, you'll understand why people thought that Powell was crazy. The footage of Class 9 rapids in *The River Wild* was a run through the sprinkler compared to what Powell took on.

But the one-armed explorer thought he could pull it off.

On May 24, 1869, Powell and a party of nine stepped into their four small boats to attempt the thousand-mile journey. Along the way, their party encountered numerous ambushes.

They were ambushed by legion killer rapids.

They were ambushed by waterfalls.

They were ambushed by boulders the size of cabins.

They were ambushed by the loss of boats, critical foodstuffs, and instruments.

Yet one hundred days later, Powell and five men emerged from two boats. All hope for their survival had been given up weeks before. They were suffering from exposure and near starvation. But they had made it.

What happened to the other four men? One had decided early on to go back. The other three, after numerous disagreements with Powell, left the expedition. They hiked up to the rim of the Canyon…only to be killed by Indians. (They should have stayed in the boat.)

COUNTRY MUSIC RESEARCH

I spent a number of hours researching John Wesley Powell's daring expedition down the Colorado. You expect to do that kind of research when you're writing a book. Just last month Mary and I were in Nashville for a conference. And when I found myself with a little free time, guess what I was doing? More research.

I was in one of the bookstores at the Opryland Hotel and came across a little book that was priceless. All it had in it were country music song titles. And some of them were absolutely classic. Here are some of my personal favorites:

- "If the Phone Doesn't Ring, It's Me"
- "There Ain't No Queen in My King-Sized Bed"
- "I've Enjoyed as Much of This as I Can Stand"
- "You're the Reason Our Kids Are Ugly"
- "Truth Is, We're Livin' a Lie"
- "I'm Ashamed to Be Here, but Not Ashamed Enough to Leave"
- "I Wouldn't Take Her to a Dogfight, Even If I Thought She Could Win"

Country music song titles are not boring. But research papers are. There is nothing quite so boring as reading research papers, and over the years I've slogged through hundreds of them. They tend to be technical, dull, and mostly out of touch with anything even remotely exciting or practical. But I recently came across a piece of research that shattered all those boring categories. Believe it or not, this research is practical, interesting, and incredibly relevant to my life and yours.

This research was done on leaders. And the reason that should be of interest to you is that, in some way, shape, or form, you *are* a leader. Are you a husband? You're a leader. Are you a dad? You're a leader. Do you teach a Sunday school class or help with a youth group? You're a leader.

Did you know that the Bible mentions over a thousand leaders? That's a lot of leaders. Some are very well known, while others scarcely get a passing mention.

Since 1982, Dr. Robert Clinton has studied almost all of these leaders.[2] Dr. Clinton has devoted his entire ministry to the study of leadership. And he has come up with some wild stuff. Over the last thirteen years, he has developed case studies on over nine hundred leaders. Some of these leaders come from the pages of Scripture, others are leaders from church history, and some are contemporary leaders. But anyway you cut it, nine hundred is a pretty thorough sample when it comes to leadership.

Clinton then reduced the nine hundred leaders to a group of one hundred whom he would characterize as prominent leaders. As he studied these one hundred leaders, Clinton was curious about something. He wanted to find out how many of those key leaders finished strong. How many of them hit the tape at full stride when they reached the end of their lives?

As he dug further in his study, he realized that of the one hundred leaders Scripture gave enough information on only forty-nine to determine how each finished. Clinton looked at those forty-nine biblical leaders and then ranked them according to how they finished. From this study, there are four different kinds of finishes that are relevant to our discussion:

- cut off early
- finished poorly
- finished "so-so"
- finished well

How do we define the various kinds of finishes? Before we take a look at Clinton's definitions, you need to keep one thing in mind. You may or may not recognize some of the names that he gives as examples. Recognizing the names is not the issue. In fact, it's no big deal if you don't recognize *any* of the names. What is important is that you understand the four basic types of finishing.

"Cut off early means they were taken out of leadership (assassinations, killed in battle, prophetically denounced, overthrown). Typical examples of those cut off early include: Abimelech, Samson, Absalom, Ahab, Josiah, John the Baptist,

and James. Some of these men were good leaders but most of them were bad."[3] Do you personally know people who have been cut off early? If you do, there is probably a tragic story that explains their finish.

"*Finished poorly* means they were going down hill in the latter part of their lives. This might mean in terms of their personal relationship with God or in terms of competency…or both. Some who…are typical examples of finishing poorly include: Gideon, Eli, Saul, and Solomon."[4] In other words, these guys were barely able to crawl across the finish line. Either that, or they were carried. This is what we want to avoid, gentlemen.

"*Finished so-so* means they did not do what they could have done or should have done. They did not complete what God had for them to do. This might mean that there were some negative ramifications (from their past) which lingered on even though they were walking with God personally at the end of their lives. Some examples of finishing so-so would be David, Jehosophat, and Hezekiah."[5] To put another spin on it, these were pretty good guys. After all, David was a man who was after God's own heart. But David really didn't finish strong. David actually finished somewhere in the middle of the pack.

"*Finished well* means that they were *walking with God personally at the end of their lives. They were strong in their faith and close to the Lord.*"[6] Clinton identifies the following men as some of those who finished well: Abraham, Job, Joseph, Joshua, Caleb, Samuel, Elijah, Jeremiah, Daniel, John, Paul, and Peter. This is where we want to be.

Now here's the big-time question. All of these leaders were gifted and all had very impressive strengths. So how come they all didn't finish strong? The answer is this. They all didn't finish strong because they didn't survive the ambushes.

Ambushes? Who said anything about ambushes?

The bottom line in determining how a man will finish centers around getting through the ambushes. To finish strong means that you survived the ambushes. Getting through the ambushes is what separates the men from the boys. And the guys who get through the ambushes are generally the guys who *anticipate the ambushes.* When John Wesley Powell stepped into the boat to begin his thousand-mile trek, he knew he wasn't going on a Carnival cruise to the Caribbean, and neither are we. So we can expect to encounter at least three major ambushes as we attempt to finish strong.

They are

- the ambush of another woman
- the ambush of money
- the ambush of a neglected family

Think through some of the men in Scripture who should have finished strong but didn't. How about Solomon, David's son? Solomon got ambushed by women. He had over seven hundred wives and three hundred concubines. No wonder he didn't finish strong. He was exhausted.

He was ambushed by money (his wealth could not even be counted), and he was ambushed by family (his foreign wives turned his heart against the Lord; see 1 Kings 11:1-8). His son Rehoboam was such a poor leader that within days of his taking the throne to replace the deceased Solomon, the people revolted and ultimately split the nation. I get the feeling Solomon didn't spend a lot of time with Rehoboam.

The enemy has been using these three ambushes to keep God's men from finishing strong for thousands of years. That's why we need to take a closer look at each one.

THE AMBUSH OF ANOTHER WOMAN

How much insurance do you have? I recently gave some thought to this question and here's what I came up with. I have health insurance, dental insurance, life insurance, disability insurance, mortgage insurance, title insurance, credit insurance, homeowner's insurance, property insurance, liability insurance, clergy malpractice insurance, car insurance, flight insurance, baggage insurance, and backup car rental insurance.

From what I've been told, when it comes to insurance, the big three are life, disability, and health. And when it comes to applying for a policy, one central issue will make or break the approval of your application.

That central issue is risk.

Risk is not only the issue in life, disability, and health, it is also the central issue in car insurance. Trust me on this one. I have just added my first teenager to our car insurance. And would you believe that my premium *doubled?*

Teenagers are at greater risk to have an accident, smokers are at greater risk to have a heart attack, men who are seriously overweight are riskier to insure than guys who keep their weight in check. That's why the insurance company always wants such a thorough physical. Quite frankly, they want to know if you are a *good* risk or a *bad* risk. But their favorite kind of risk is known as a "preferred risk."

Risk is also the central issue in determining whether or not you will survive the ambush of another woman. Do you remember the study that Dr. Howard Hendricks conducted that I mentioned in chapter one? Dr. Hendricks interviewed each of 246 men in full-time ministry who experienced moral failure within a two-year period of time. In other words, Prof Hendricks was able to find nearly 250 men who without a doubt were committed to Jesus Christ. Yet the thing they had in common was that within twenty-four months of each other they each got involved in sexual immorality. In other words, here are nearly 250 Christian men who got suckered into the ambush of another woman!

After interviewing each man, Dr. Hendricks discovered four correlations running through the experiences of the entire 246 who derailed:

- None were involved in any kind of personal accountability group.

- Each had ceased to invest in a daily personal time of prayer, Scripture reading, and worship.

- Over 80 percent of them became sexually involved with another woman as the result of counseling the woman. In other words, they were spending significant portions of their schedules with women other than their wives.

- Without exception, each of the 246 had been convinced that moral failure "will never happen to me."[7]

You know what's fascinating about these 246 guys? Every one of them was high risk. No one in their right mind would have looked at these guys and insured them against getting involved with another woman. Do you know why? They were doing everything to insure that they *would* get involved! Not one of those guys could be considered a "preferred" risk. And every one of them went down.

If you want to find out if you're high risk for car insurance, you check your driving record. If you want to get a new life insurance policy, the company will want to know if you are a good risk or a bad risk, so they will send you to a doctor to get a physical.

When it comes to finishing strong, you can actually rate yourself. No kidding. Just answer these four simple questions:

1. Do you spend personal time with the Lord in prayer and reading Scripture at least three times a week?

2. Are there at least one or two men in your life with whom you have built a friendship based on trust, confidentiality, and accountability? In other words, do you have a buddy who is close enough (that means you can't con him) and loves you enough to get in your face if he needs to?

3. Are you currently spending significant time with any attractive woman other than your wife (a woman you work with, a woman you are counseling, etc.)?

4. Are you absolutely sure that you will finish strong?

Let's go back over those questions one more time, and this time we will supply the answer that is necessary to be a "preferred risk."

1. Do you spend personal time with the Lord in prayer and reading Scripture at least three times a week? Correct answer: YES.

2. Are there at least one or two men in your life with whom you have built

a friendship based on trust, confidentiality, and accountability? Correct answer: YES.

3. Are you currently spending significant time with any attractive woman other than your wife? Correct answer: NO.

4. Are you absolutely sure that you will finish strong? Correct answer: NO.

If you have one wrong answer, you are at risk. If you have two wrong answers, you are a moderate risk. If you have three wrong answers, you are a bad risk. If you have four wrong answers, you are dead meat.

Why would I say that you are dead meat if you have four wrong answers? Because each of the 246 men who got involved in sexual immorality gave the same four answers that you did. It's not a matter of *if* it will happen to you, it's a matter of *when*.

In the last ten years, some very high-profile evangelists have stumbled into an ambush. Specifically, they wandered into the ambush of another woman.

Millie Dienert has worked with the Billy Graham team for forty years. Her comments on the ethics of Mr. Graham, Cliff Barrows, George Beverly Shea, and the rest of the male members of the team make the point:

> I have always appreciated, from a moral point of view, how the men
> have been in their attitude toward the secretaries. The doors are always
> left open. There is a high regard for the lack of any kind of privacy
> where a boss and his secretary are involved. At times, I thought they
> were going a little too far, that it wasn't necessary, but I'm glad they did
> it, especially today. They have kept everything above reproach. When
> you are working on a long-term basis with the same person,
> constantly, in hotels, where the wife is not there and the secretary is,
> that is a highly explosive situation. You have to take precautions. I
> have always respected the way they have handled that. It has been
> beautifully done.[8]

What a remarkable compliment. When it comes to avoiding the ambush of another woman, that's the kind of record we need to shoot for.

THE AMBUSH OF MONEY

I heard a story the other day about three retired guys sitting on the beach in Florida.

"What kind of business were you in?" the first guy asked the second.

"I had an electronics manufacturing company up north, and we did real well for a number of years. But then the competition got real tough from the Orient. I was thinking about selling, but then my water pipes burst and ruined all my machinery and flooded the factory. Everything was ruined. I retired and came down here on the insurance money. How about you?"

"I had a box company in Maine," the first guy said, "and things were going great. Then the price of materials shot up and stayed there—it nearly ruined me! A fire destroyed my entire operation last year. Fortunately, my insurance covered everything, and that's when we decided to move down here and get out of the business."

The third guy then said, "I had a clothing factory in Puerto Rico and we were getting by. But then the manufacturers from China, with their cheap labor costs, just about drove me into bankruptcy. I just couldn't compete with their prices. Then a hurricane blew in and annihilated not only my plant but my house. I collected the insurance and decided to come to Florida."

The other two guys looked at each other.

"How do you make a hurricane?" they asked.

I know a guy with a Ph. D. in theology from one of the leading theological institutions in the world. He's also a convicted felon who is currently sitting in a federal prison for ripping off a number of savings and loans in a real estate scam. The interesting thing about this guy is that he has systematic theology wired. And he can explain to you all the nuances of a biblical passage from the Hebrew or the Greek.

So how does a young biblical expert wind up in prison? He has a weakness for money. Now this guy didn't start with scamming money in real estate deals. He started by fooling around with deductions on his income tax return. Nothing big. Just a few hundred here and a few hundred there. He never had a problem with cutting just a few corners on his return. And when he got his real estate license, he never found a deal that he couldn't fix with a little creative financing.

Ananias thought he was pretty good at creative financing, too. And his story is told in the Book of Acts.

> But a certain man named Ananias, with his wife Sapphira, sold a piece
> of property, and kept back some of the price for himself, with his wife's
> full knowledge, and bringing a portion of it, he laid it at the apostles'
> feet. But Peter said, "Ananias, why has Satan filled your heart to lie to
> the Holy Spirit, and to keep back some of the price of the land?
> While it remained unsold, did it not remain your own? And after it
> was sold, was it not under your control? Why is it that you have
> conceived this deed in your heart? You have not lied to men, but to
> God." And as he heard these words, Ananias fell down and breathed
> his last; and great fear came upon all who heard of it. And the young
> men arose and covered him up, and after carrying him out, they
> buried him. (Acts 5:1–6)

Ananias had what could be called a "premature finish." But it wasn't just Ananias.

> Now there elapsed an interval of about three hours, and his wife came
> in, not knowing what had happened. And Peter responded to her, "Tell
> me whether you sold the land for such and such a price?" And she
> said, "Yes, that was the price." Then Peter said to her, "Why is it that
> you have agreed together to put the Spirit of the Lord to the test?
> Behold, the feet of those who have buried your husband are at the

door, and they shall carry you out as well." And she fell immediately at his feet, and breathed her last; and the young men came in and found her dead, and they carried her out and buried her beside her husband. And great fear came upon the whole church, and upon all who heard of these things. (Acts 5: 7–11)

Does great fear come upon you when you hear of Ananias and Sapphira? It should.

Awhile back I heard a preacher on TV declaring that what the church needs today is a return to the Book of Acts. And then he listed the wonderful healings in the Book of Acts and all the special manifestations of the Holy Spirit in the Book of Acts. And every time he would list one of the miracles of God that's recorded in Acts, he would follow with the line, "What the church today needs is a return to the Book of Acts!"

I think this guy is on to something. But there's one thing that makes me a little nervous.

He never mentioned Ananias and Sapphira. And if we're going to return to the Book of Acts, we'll have to take the whole book—not just the exciting parts. If we ever do return to those days, a lot of churches will have to convert part of their parking lots to cemetery plots. Why? Because the ambush of money is still with us today.

If Ananias and Sapphira had such a love for money, then why did they give any money to the church in the first place? The answer is in Acts 4:34–37, the verses immediately prior to their own story:

> For there was not a needy person among them, for all who were owners of lands or houses would sell them and bring the proceeds of the sales, and lay them at the apostles' feet; and they would be distributed to each, as any had need.
>
> And Joseph, a Levite of Cyprian birth, who was also called Barnabas by the apostles (which translated means, Son of

Encouragement), and who owned a tract of land, sold it and brought the money and laid it at the apostles' feet.

Two things come to mind here. First of all, Ananias and Sapphira were more interested in looking good than in doing good. The second is a question. Do you think this event was the first time that this couple had ever lied about something related to their finances?

How are you doing with the ambush of money? Are you shooting straight with people when it comes to money? Or are you falsifying loan applications or tax returns? Have you misled someone recently in order to profit financially? If so, the enemy is setting you up. I don't know how much you stand to make off the deal, but let me tell you this. No matter how much it is, it just isn't worth it. At least, not if you want to finish strong.

Henry Fielding was right. "If you make money your god, it will plague you like the devil."

THE AMBUSH OF A NEGLECTED FAMILY

I don't know why I remember this so clearly, but I do. Twenty-four years ago, I was on summer vacation from seminary. I was walking with a friend from the campus of UCLA to the Sizzler steak house in Westwood. As we were walking, he asked me a question.

"Steve, what's your greatest fear about going into ministry?"

I didn't hesitate with my answer. "Being successful in ministry and losing my family."

When I answered that question, I wasn't married and I didn't have kids. But even as a single guy I knew that when I did marry and have kids, I didn't want to lose them in some ambush.

Why was I so concerned—even at that stage of my life? I was concerned because *every pastor that I had known to that point*—except for one—had seen his kids tube their faith once they got out of the house.

I have grown up in the world of evangelical Christianity. I am very grateful for that heritage. To be raised from birth with a view of life in which Jesus Christ and the Scriptures are central to all of life is an incredible privilege.

I have one small criticism, however, about evangelical Christianity, and it is this. We tend sometimes to confuse spirituality with weirdness. And the weirder the behavior, the more "spiritual" it must be.

C. T. Studd is a highly revered name in our Christian heritage. In his day, Studd was the most famous cricket player in all of England. He came from a tremendously wealthy family but gave away his entire inheritance and then went to the mission field. He served for a number of years in China and then returned to England. Several years later he felt called to go to Africa.

And he went.

By himself.

C. T. Studd didn't see his wife again for seventeen years. *Seventeen years.* Can you believe that? I'm sorry, but that's weird. That's not spiritual, that's strange. Especially when Paul makes it so clear in 1 Corinthians 9:5 that the apostles who were married did take their wives with them as they ministered: "Do we not have a right to take along a believing wife, even as the rest of the apostles, and the brothers of the Lord, and Cephas [Peter]?"

If the apostles took their wives, the brothers of Jesus took their wives, and Peter took his wife with him, then how come old C. T. didn't take his wife? Was he more spiritual than the apostles? Did he have an edge on Peter? Should he be held up as the role model for the rest of us to emulate? It sounds to me more like the ambush of a neglected family.

I like my wife. I like to be with my wife. She's good-looking, she's smart, and I like to hang out with her. I like to go to Chili's and eat chips and hot sauce with my wife. I have no interest in not seeing my wife for seventeen years. Listen…I have no interest in not seeing my wife for seventeen *days.*

William Carey left England in 1793 to go to India to preach the gospel. He took his wife with him. Adoniram Judson went from America to Burma in

1814. He took his wife with him. Robert Morrison was the first Protestant missionary to go to China. He took his wife with him.

These men knew the dangers they were facing. They knew there would be deficient diets, poor nutrition, and minimal medical care. And all of them lost family members on the mission field. *But better to face the adversity together as a family than to neglect one another through a distorted understanding of Christ's demands on one's family.*

Recently I was in the library at Dallas Theological Seminary doing further research on country music titles (just kidding). Actually, I was looking for the biography of a particular man who had been greatly used by God earlier in this century. As I reached for the book, I noticed the two biographies that were on either side of it. Each of those biographies was also about a man who had made a great impact for Christ earlier in this century. I was familiar with both of their stories, and that's when it hit me in a split second. All three of those men who had been so successful in reaching hundreds of thousands for Christ had lost their own families.

- One spent an average of ten months away from home each year for fifteen years. He led thousands to Christ, but his oldest daughter committed suicide, and his marriage ended in divorce.
- One of the men was famous for his preaching ability, and he traveled constantly all over the United States, accepting invitations. One of his sons grew up to become one of the first public figures to unashamedly declare his homosexuality and rejection of Christianity.
- One of the men was an incredibly gifted evangelist who faithfully preached the gospel to his dying day. His wife was the administrative genius who organized his city-wide meetings across America. They had four young children who were raised by a nanny since their mother was on the road with their father and not available to them the vast majority of the time. One of this man's dying regrets was that his sons would have *nothing* to do with his parents' Christianity. I wonder why.

I think it is entirely possible that those very well-meaning people got drawn off by the enemy into the ambush of a neglected family. And it severely affected the way that each of them finished.

Jesus asked the question, "For what should it profit a man if he should gain the whole world and lose his own soul?" Another question is also worth pondering: "What shall it profit a man if he should win the whole world and lose his own family?"

Some would say that the sacrifice these men made should be held up as an ideal for the rest of us. I want to be fair to these men. They loved Jesus Christ and faithfully preached His Word. Their motivation was to further the kingdom at any cost. But let's also be fair to their children. Does Christ give a man a wife and children and then ask him to willfully neglect them? That makes no sense. It is not consistent with the character of God. It is not consistent with the tender Father-heart of God who said, "I will never leave you nor forsake you."

I can hear the pages rustling as someone turns to Luke 14:26 where Jesus said, "If anyone comes to Me, and does not hate his own father and mother and wife and children and brothers and sisters, yes, and even his own life, he cannot be My disciple."

Do you remember when God told Abraham to take young Isaac up to Mount Moriah and sacrifice him? Abraham had waited until he was one hundred years old to receive a son from the Lord, and now that same Lord was going to take him away. Genesis 22 tells the story that grips the heart of every father. At one point, as they were making their way up the mountain and young Isaac was toting the wood for the sacrifice, he asked his father where the lamb for the sacrifice was. Abraham replied with what had to be a broken heart that God would provide the sacrifice. You know the story.

Abraham built an altar, and then he carefully laid out the wood and tied Isaac on top of the altar. Before his young son could speak, he raised his knife and thrust it into Isaac's heart. And as Abraham stood over the body of his lifeless son, a voice came out of heaven and said, "Well done, good and faithful servant!"

But that's not what happened, is it? As Abraham raised the knife to bring it down upon Isaac, the angel of the Lord called out to Abraham and said, "Wait a minute!" Actually he didn't say "wait a minute." But that's what he meant.

> But the angel of the LORD called to him from heaven, and said, "Abraham, Abraham!" And he said, "Here I am." And he said, "Do not stretch out your hand against the lad, and do nothing to him; for now I know that you fear God, since you have not withheld your son, your only son, from Me." (Genesis 22:11–12)

And then Abraham saw a ram caught in the thicket, and there was their sacrifice.

So what was God doing? Well, verse one of this same chapter very clearly teaches that God was testing Abraham. What God wanted to know was whether or not He was Number One in Abraham's life. And that's what Jesus was saying in Luke 14:26. Abraham was being tested to find out if he loved his son more than he loved God. Our children cannot be our gods. Our wives cannot be our gods.

Only God can be our God.

He wants to know that He is first in our lives. And there are times that He will test us in various ways to make sure that He has His rightful place. But it doesn't mean that God is in the business of killing children on Mount Moriah—or killing families in the 1990s, for that matter.

If ever a man was sold out to the Lord, it was D. L. Moody. And here's what Moody had to say about all of this: "I believe the family was established long before the church, and that my duty is to my family first. I am not to neglect my family." I think that Moody would like what John Barnett had to say about being a dad. Barnett captured the essence of being a dad when he wrote these words to his nearly grown-up son:

> After getting my first chance to change your diaper, I brought you back downstairs. I turned on the television and as luck would have it, the

San Francisco 49ers were playing.... I turned out all the lights, lay
down on the couch, and put you on my chest. I was so afraid that my
big hands were going to drop you, but I held on. It wasn't five minutes
later that you fell asleep, holding my finger.... It was at that moment I
realized that I was a dad.[9]

That's not weird. That's great. And I will guarantee you that Barnett's experience brought pleasure to God.

Why do I say that? Because the very last thing that God said in the Old Testament was this:

And he will restore the hearts of the fathers to their children, and the hearts
of the children to their fathers, lest I come and smite the land with a curse.
(Malachi 4:6)

God did not give any more revelation after that verse for four hundred years. And when John the Baptist eventually came on the scene, he not only was the forerunner of Jesus Christ, but he preached a message that would restore the hearts of the fathers to their children (see Luke 1:13–17).

In 1 Timothy 5:8, God declares that a man who will not provide for his family is worse than a pagan. Most would agree that the reference is to financial provision. But if God is that concerned about the financial provision that a man would give to his family, would He not be more concerned that a man give emotional and spiritual provision as well?

God is not in the business of asking us to consistently neglect our families in order to further His kingdom. As a matter of fact, the Scripture teaches that if a man is not adequately meeting the needs of his family, he is disqualified from having a ministry (1 Timothy 3:4, 5).

In other words, a man is only to be given a public ministry after he has first proven his leadership abilities with his own family. If he fails to take care of his family, then as far as God is concerned, he is not qualified to take on any other kind of ministry. And that, friend, is one of the single most violated principles in the Church of Jesus Christ.

"Yes," someone says, "he's having family problems. But...the man is so *gifted!*"

Yes, but the qualification for having a public ministry is not *giftedness.* The qualification for ministry is *proven character.* A gifted man is not necessarily a mature man. In fact, gifted men are often less mature than their peers precisely *because* they are so gifted. As a result, things tend to come easily to them. They haven't had to work as hard or discipline themselves as much as others around them have had to do. And that's why gifted men often lag behind in character.

Someone else says, "Isn't it necessary at times to neglect one's family in order to fulfill the Great Commission?" But what is the Great Commission? Jesus said this to his disciples: "Go therefore and make disciples of all the nations, baptizing them in the name of the Father and the Son and the Holy Spirit, teaching them to observe all that I commanded you." (Matthew 28:19–20).

I don't care if you are an accountant, a truckdriver, a computer programmer, a pastor, or an architect. If you have a family (or even if you don't), it is your job to fulfill the Great Commission. And the heart of the Great Commission is to make disciples. And that, friend, starts in our own homes. You don't have to sell your business and go to China to fulfill the Great Commission. But you do need to make sure you're getting home in time to hang out with your wife and kids.

It takes time to make disciples. That's why I recently turned down an invitation to speak in Australia for a month. The schedule and itinerary were all set and it would take me to every major city in Australia to address Christian men about the importance of leading and discipling their families. Why did I turn down such a fabulous opportunity?

I turned it down because I couldn't take my family with me. They wanted me to come in March—when my kids are in school. If we could have worked something out for the summer, I would have gone. But someone might say, "It's only for a month." That's true. But my daughter leaves for college in less than two years, and quite frankly I don't want to be away from her for a month. That time is extremely valuable to me.

I find it somewhat ironic that I should go to Australia and leave my own family in order to instruct other men as to how they can disciple their own families. That just doesn't add up to me. My youngest son will be heading off to college in eight years. That's when I would thoroughly enjoy going to Australia for a month…with Mary.

Jesus accepted numerous speaking opportunities…but He apparently always took His disciples with Him. I think that I should pretty much follow His example. If He took His disciples with Him, then I should take my disciples with me. I don't usually call them disciples, but that's what they are. And your kids are your disciples. Jesus took His disciples with Him when He would go somewhere to speak, and the apostles would take their wives when they went off to preach. So let's not get weird, guys. If you can take your wife along on a business trip, take her. If you can take your kids, take 'em!

Make sure that you get home from work in time for dinner. And if you don't ever have time to coach one of your son's or daughter's teams, then you're getting weird. Real weird. If God should call you to use your gifts and abilities in another country and culture, then go for it. But don't go by yourself.

We can be intimidated by stupid expectations from the church, and we can be intimidated by stupid expectations at our jobs. Life is too short. Those kids will be gone before you know it. Your opportunity to mold and shape their lives will be gone forever. Don't let the enemy sucker you into working excessive hours to give your kids more things. Your kids don't need more things. They need you. And they want you. The more time that you can spend with them, the more they are going to want to be like you and know the heavenly Father who made you such a great dad. That's how you lead your kids to Christ.

The ambush of a neglected family is a very real ambush. There are all kinds of bullets out there that can kill a man's priorities and cause him to neglect his family. That's why so many kids in your neighborhood don't have dads.

Somebody shot their Pa.

For some, it's the bullet that flies out of the ambush of another woman.

For others, it's the ambush of money.

And some go down because of the ambush of a neglected family.

But whatever the ambush may be, I'll guarantee you this.

It's no laughing matter.

CHAPTER THREE

STAYING THE COURSE

————•

Untutored courage is useless
in the face of educated bullets.

GEORGE S. PATTON JR.

Willie and Ray, a couple of ranchers, met at the feed store one afternoon. "Had some problems with my herd," said Willie. "My prize bull was impotent. But the vet came over and gave him some special medicine and now he seems to be doing just fine."

Several weeks later Willie and Ray met again at the store.

"Hey, Willie," said Ray, "now *my* bull is having problems. What was that medicine the vet prescribed?"

"I don't remember the name," Willie said. "But it kinda tastes like chocolate."

Hey, we all need a little strong medicine now and then, don't we? In the movie *City Slickers,* a poignant scene occurs between Jack Palance and Billy Crystal; Palance is giving Crystal some strong medicine for life that he doesn't want to take. I've borrowed this scene from *Halftime*, Bob Buford's excellent book for men:

> Palance and Crystal are riding slowly across the range on horseback,
> discussing life and love. Palance plays a wily cowpoke, while Crystal is

a tenderfoot from Los Angeles who has paid for a two-week dude ranch vacation. Of course, he gets more than he bargained for, and in the process, Crystal learns something important about himself.[1]

Palance: Cowboy leads a different kind of life. When there were cowboys. They're a dying breed. Still means something to me, though. In a couple of days, we'll move this herd across the river, drive them through the valley. Ahhh, there's nothing like bringing in the herd.

Crystal: You see, that's great. Your life makes sense to you.

Palance: (Laughs)

Crystal: What? What's so funny?

Palance: You city folk. You worry a lot, don't you?... How old are you? Thirty-eight?

Crystal: Thirty-nine.

Palance: Yeah. You all come out here about the same age. Same problems. Spend fifty weeks a year getting knots in your rope then— then you think two weeks up here will untie them for you. None of you get it. (Long pause) Do you know what the secret of life is?

Crystal: No, what?

Palance: This. (Holds up his index finger)

Crystal: Your finger?

Palance: ONE THING. Just one thing. You stick to that and nothing else matters.

Crystal: That's great, but what's the one thing?

Palance: That's what you've got to figure out.[2]

Have you got it figured out? What is the "one thing"?

I'll do better than that old cowboy. I'll tell you what it is: It's *finishing strong.*

The greatest thing you can leave behind is the example of a life well lived. If you leave that to your kids, then you've left them *everything.* It may not be what Jack Palance had in mind, but it's sure as heck what I have in mind. And so do you. Otherwise you wouldn't have read this far.

I like the way Paul put it, somewhere in the last half of his race:

> I don't mean to say I am perfect. I haven't learned all I should even yet,
> but I keep working toward that day when I will finally be all that
> Christ saved me for and wants me to be.
>
> No, dear brothers, I am still not all I should be but I am bringing
> all my energies to bear on this one thing: Forgetting the past and
> looking forward to what lies ahead, I strain to reach the end of the race
> and receive the prize for which God is calling us up to heaven because
> of what Christ Jesus did for us. (Philippians 3:12–14, TLB)

That was Paul's "one thing." Forgetting the past and straining toward that finish line with all of his strength. I've always liked those verses, but at this particular point in my life, those words hit me hard...right in the gut.

A PERSONAL MISSION STATEMENT

Last month I turned forty-five years old. You can slice that any you want, but it always comes out "middle age." Like it or not, forty-five is in the middle of aging. It's right there between birth and ninety. Forty-five is hard for me to believe. Just a few years ago I was twenty-five. Now I'm forty-five. In a few more years, I'll be sixty-five.

It's an appropriate exercise for a man who finds himself at middle age (or to use the more palatable term, mid-life) to evaluate how he's doing, now that he's reached the halfway point of the journey. Not only is it good to evaluate the years you've already lived, but it's very wise to consider how you want to spend the rest of your life.

In *The Seven Habits of Highly Effective People*, Steven Covey discusses the importance of having a personal mission statement. A mission statement is a document a person writes that sums up his or her personal philosophy or creed.

ns it to the United States Constitution. The Constitution is the stan-

ur nation. A personal mission statement should articulate the values
that represent the person.

As an example, Covey quotes the personal mission statement of his friend
Rolfe Kerr. Here are some of the things Kerr included:

- Succeed at home first.
- Never compromise with honesty.
- Hear both sides before judging.
- Obtain the counsel of others.
- Defend those who are absent.
- Develop one new proficiency a year.
- Plan tomorrow's work today.
- Maintain a positive attitude.
- Keep a sense of humor.
- Be orderly in person and in work.
- Listen twice as much as you speak.
- Concentrate all abilities and efforts on the task at hand, not worrying about the next job or promotion.[3]

That's not a bad piece of work. It's a statement that reflects the values and philosophy of how one man wants to live his life.

Personal mission statements are important documents. That's why some people spend days—even weeks—developing a mission statement unique to them. Some executives have been known to spend thousands of dollars to go off on their own to some remote, exotic hideaway to think about life and hammer out a personal mission statement.

Several years ago, as I was edging gingerly through the door of mid-life, I decided to come up with a mission statement of my own. I'd been reflecting a bit about the first half of my life, and I was doing some hard thinking about the second part. You may find this odd, but it didn't take me several days to come up with my mission statement. It didn't even take a day. I didn't even have to go away to some island or retreat center to think about it.

Quite frankly, it took me about two minutes.

I've had this mission statement for over four years now. Covey says it's not unusual for a person to modify or amend his mission statement as time goes by. Yet my statement is going on five years old, and I haven't changed one word of the original two-minute composition. Here it is.

——Don't screw up.——

That's it. It's not real long, it's not real sophisticated, it's not real polished, and it's not real religious. But it is *real*. As I look over the rest of my life, I don't want to screw up. Do you? Of course, you don't. I don't know any man who wants to screw up. Yet men screw up all the time. My goal for the second half of my life is not to screw up in a major way.

- I don't want to screw up my marriage.

- I don't want to screw up my relationship with my kids.

- I don't want to screw up my integrity.

One day in the future there will be a funeral. My funeral. After the funeral, they'll get in the black limos and head for the cemetery where a brief graveside service will be conducted. Then everyone will head to the house and have some food.

As my family and friends are eating at the house, the workers at the cemetery will be using a small tractor to dump dirt over my casket and put the sod back in place over the fresh grave. In another day or so, another worker will lay the marker over the grave. Usually a marker will have people's names and the dates of their birth and death. It's also common to have a few final words inscribed on the marker.

Have you ever given any thought to what you'd like to have inscribed on your grave marker? I have. It would be fine with me if my grave marker read like this:

Steven James Farrar

Born: 1949

Died: ——

He Didn't Screw Up

I wouldn't mind it at all if someone chiseled those words in granite underneath my name. Do you know why? Because it would mean I finished strong. It's like a coin with a head and a tail. On one side is "Finish Strong." On the flip side is "Don't Screw Up."

We've already established the fact that none of us is perfect. All of us fall short every day as husbands and fathers. At least I can vouch for the fact that I do. What I have in mind is avoiding the *major* screwups of life. Guys who screw up are guys who willfully and purposefully remove themselves from the protection of Jesus Christ.

There's no reason in the world that any of us shouldn't finish strong. I don't care what the odds are, you and I don't have to go down. Old Peter laid it on the line as clear as can be just a short time before his brief appointment with the executioner. Knowing he was just about to hit life's finish line, the big fisherman scratched out these words:

> His divine power has given us everything we need for life and godliness through our knowledge of him who called us by his own glory and goodness. Through these he has given us his very great and precious promises, so that through them you may participate in the divine nature and escape the corruption in the world caused by evil desires. (2 Peter 1:3–4, NIV)

Did you catch that? We've been given *everything we need* for life and godliness. So why is it that so many guys who've been given everything still don't finish strong? It's because they *choose* to step out from under the Lord's protection and power.

Those ten guys with Joshua and Caleb could have finished strong. But they *chose* to step out from under His protection. They had a greater fear of man than they did of God.

John Bisagno listed the names of twenty-four young men who were tracking with Christ in their twenties. Yet thirty years later, only three of those twenty-four were still truckin'. All of those twenty-four guys could have finished strong. But twenty-one of them *chose* to remove themselves from His protection and power.

An old parable told by a Haitian pastor makes the point.

A certain man wanted to sell his house for two thousand dollars. Another man wanted to buy it very badly, but he was a poor man and didn't have the full price. After much bargaining, the owner agreed to sell the house to the man for one thousand dollars. But the reduced price came with a stipulation. The owner would sell the house, but he would keep ownership of a large nail protruding from over the front door.

Several years later, the original owner decided he wanted to buy the house back. Understandably, the new owner was unwilling to sell. As a result, the original owner went out, found the carcass of a dead dog in the street, and hung it from the nail he still owned. Soon the house became unlivable, and the family was forced to sell to the owner of the nail.

The Haitian pastor concluded the story: "If we leave the devil with even one small peg in our life, he will return to hang his rotting garbage on it."[4]

You may own the entire home, but if you give the enemy access to just one nail in your life, it definitely puts you in the high risk bracket.

Let me ask you something. Is there a nail over the front door of your life? A nail that you have leased out to the enemy? If there is, you need to deed it over to Christ. Now.

TWENTY-FOUR STABILIZING NAILS

In the last five years, a truckload of Christian books have been written for men. I find that kind of humorous because I remember talking with some publishers seven years ago and discussing my idea of writing a book to men. They were very gracious and certainly didn't want to discourage me, but they did point out that seven out of ten buyers in a typical Christian bookstore are women, and the idea of writing a book just to men was probably not a very good idea from a marketing standpoint.

I recently came across a book to men that was not written in the last five years. It was written in 1666. Without a doubt, this was the original Christian men's book. This guy was doing Promise Keepers over three hundred years ago. The title is *The Godly Man's Picture,* by Thomas Watson. Once you work your way through the King James language, it's a superb book. Watson gives twenty-four characteristics of a godly man. I like to think of these as twenty-four stabilizing nails that you can hammer into the character of your life.

According to Watson, a godly man is

1. a man of knowledge
2. a man moved by faith
3. a man fired by love
4. a man like God
5. a man careful about the worship of God
6. a man who serves God, not men
7. a man who prizes Christ
8. a man who weeps
9. a man who loves the Word
10. a man who has the Spirit of God residing in him
11. a man of humility
12. a man of prayer
13. a man of sincerity
14. a heavenly man
15. a zealous man
16. a patient man
17. a thankful man

18. a man who loves the saints

19. a man who does not indulge himself in any sin

20. a man who is good in his relationships

21. a man who does spiritual things in a spiritual manner

22. a man thoroughly trained in religion

23. a man who walks with God

24. a man who strives to be an instrument for making others godly

Watson devotes almost two hundred pages of amazingly small print to explain each of the twenty-four characteristics. And he comes up with a dynamite conclusion. This is Thomas Watson's "one thing."

His conclusion is that "these characteristics are a Christian's box of evidences." Of this kind of man, Watson says, "*He is as sure to go to heaven as if he were in heaven already.*" I love that statement. That's another way of saying this guy isn't going to "just finish." He's going to finish strong. And why is this guy going to finish strong? Because, as the old hymn puts it, he is "stayed upon Jehovah." I've always loved that line. Stayed upon Jehovah. That's got some meat in it.

I don't know about you, but I have an attention deficit disorder. That means I sometimes have trouble concentrating and focusing on the task at hand. And there's no way in the cotton pickin' world that a guy with ADD is going to remember those twenty-four traits. By the time I get to number seven, I'm already thinking about what we're going to have for dinner tonight. I can't remember twenty-four, but I can remember *four*. And so can you.

So here's what I've come up with to help me finish strong.

Guys who finish strong are stayed upon Jehovah.

And guys who are stayed upon Jehovah consistently do four things:

- *They stay in.*

- *They stay close.*

- *They stay away.*

- *They stay alert.*

Now if I can remember those four "stays," then you can remember them. Even if you have attention deficit disorder.

In the last chapter we looked at some of the ambushes that can prevent us from finishing strong. But we need something more. If you and I are going to keep from being ambushed, we need a simple plan. These four "stays" are a simple, sure-fire plan. They enable us to *anticipate* and *avoid* the ambushes. Let's go to it.

STAY IN ... THE SCRIPTURES

Stay in...what? Stay in the *Scriptures*. The first absolute requirement for finishing strong is to stay in the Word of God. The term used throughout the Bible for this exercise is "meditation."

When Joshua was handed the reins to the nation of Israel, here's what God told him to do:

> "This book of the law shall not depart from your mouth, but you shall *meditate* on it day and night, so that you may be careful to do according to all that is written in it; for then you will make your way prosperous, and then you will have success. Have I not commanded you? Be strong and courageous! Do not tremble or be dismayed, for the LORD your God is with you wherever you go." (Joshua 1:8–9)

You may be thinking, "That's great for Joshua, but I've got a company to run! I can't think about the Bible all day long. I've got people to manage, ledgers to balance, and decisions to make. This sounds good, but it just isn't practical!"

Let me assure you that meditation is the most practical thing in the world. Joshua didn't sit around all day thinking about every detail of God's law. He had two million people to manage. He had to figure out a way to feed them, protect them, and mobilize them for battle. Joshua was as busy, if not more so, than you are. So how in the world does a busy man meditate on the Bible? It's easy.

The Lord told Joshua, "This book…shall not depart from your mouth."

In other words, *you just put a pinch between your cheek and gum.*

Years ago, Walt Garrison, former fullback for the Dallas Cowboys, did a series of television commercials for a brand of smokeless tobacco. And Walt's famous line was, "You just put a pinch between your cheek and gum." I am convinced that the same principle applies to staying in the Word of God.

Let me show you what I mean.

I like to read over a book of the Bible several times to get a feel for it. Let's say that several times a week you have some private time with the Lord to read the Scriptures. Let's say you're going to zero in on the book of 1 Timothy. Now you can read the book of 1 Timothy in about twenty or thirty minutes. If you don't have thirty minutes to read the whole book, that's okay. Read the first half of the book one morning, and the second half the next morning. But as you read through the book, you'll come across some specific verses that jump out at you. They apply to a situation or a decision you have to make. You may have seen these verses scores of times before, but now they seem to rise off the page as if they were in bold print or neon green. When that happens, you want to mark that verse. Use a highlighter or a pen, but do something to make that verse stand out.

Every time you come across a verse like that, mark it! And I would suggest that you read through the book several times, giving the Holy Spirit the opportunity to point things out to you.

Next, take those highlighted verses and write them down on a three-by-five card or a sticky note. Put one on the dash of your car, put another in your datebook, slide another into your shirt pocket, and stick yet another on your bathroom mirror so that you'll see it when you shave. After a while that verse is going to become real familiar to you. Why? Because when you go into the bathroom, you put a pinch of Scripture between your cheek and gum. When you get in the car, you've got another pinch. When you look at your appointment book, you've got another pinch. When you're on the NordicTrack, you take another pinch. When you're waiting in line at the grocery store, you pull the verse out of your pocket and you've got one more pinch. Do you get my drift here?

As you go through the day, you've always got the Word of God in your cheek and you're chewing on it. You're getting the juice and flavor out of it. That's meditation. One guy put it this way in Psalm 119:11: "Thy word I have put in my cheek that I may not sin against Thee."

Actually, he said, "Thy word I have treasured in my heart, that I may not sin against Thee," but the idea is exactly the same.

As you go about your day, you are always—consciously or subconsciously— chewing on the Word of God. And then from time to time during the day, you'll come up against temptation. You will be tempted to lie, you will be tempted to lust, you will be tempted to tell a client that a check is in the mail when you know full well that it isn't in the mail. So what do you do when you are tempted?

You spit.

When you suddenly face some kind of temptation, you immediately spit the Word of God right into the eye of that temptation. And that's how you beat it. But if you don't have a pinch between your cheek and gum, you've got nothing to spit. That's why men who finish strong are guys who chew God's truth all day long. It works! Try it for a week and see if it doesn't help you fight off temptation. You chew, you spit, and guess what? You finish the day strong. And at the end of all days, you finish life strong.

STAY CLOSE ... TO A FRIEND

Stay close...to a friend you can't con. Stay close to a friend who loves you enough to tell you when you're screwing up. Stay close to a friend who will never violate a confidence. That's the kind of friend we all need.

The hot word right now in Christian circles is "accountability." And it ought to be hot. Accountability is a good thing when it is experienced within biblical parameters.

One of the primary ways that the enemy keeps a guy from finishing strong is isolation. Instead of being close to anyone, you become distant. Instead of being gut-level honest, you begin to shade the truth. And instead of following Christ you begin to *act* like you are following Christ. That's what happens when a guy gets isolated and tries to go one-on-one with Satan.

Dr. James Houston observed:

> Sin always tends to make us blind to our own faults. We need a friend
> to stop us from deceiving ourselves that what we are doing is not so
> bad after all. We need a friend to help us overcome our low self-image,
> inflated self-importance, selfishness, pride, our deceitful nature, our
> dangerous fantasies and so much else.[5]

Here are a couple of verses I've tucked between my cheek and gum for a number of years:

> See to it, brothers, that none of you has a sinful, unbelieving heart that
> turns away from the living God. But *encourage one another daily,* as long
> as it is called Today, so that none of you may be hardened by sin's
> deceitfulness. (Hebrews 3:12–13, NIV)

Do you see the implication there? If you don't have encouragement—even daily encouragement—you could be deceived by sin. You could get hard and begin to turn away from the Lord. This kind of friendship isn't a luxury, it's a necessity.

Roy Rogers had Pat Brady. Gene Autry had Gabby Hayes. Matt Dillon had Chester. The Lone Ranger had Tonto. Batman had Robin. Superman had nobody.

Maybe you've heard the story about Muhammad Ali back when he was the reigning heavyweight champion of the world. Ali had just taken his seat in the first-class section of a 747 that was getting ready to take off. The flight attendant came by and asked the champ to fasten his seat belt.

Ali looked at the woman and said, "Superman don't need no seat belt."

The attendant responded, "Superman don't need no plane."

Guess what? You're not Superman, and I'm not either. And if you are trying to fly by yourself, then the enemy has you seriously deceived.

But I don't have a friend, you may be thinking. Then ask God to give you one. And be willing to take that first step and *become* a friend to someone when God answers your prayer and gives you that little nudge.

About thirteen years ago, I got blindsided by a major depression. I had never dealt with depression before in my life. In fact, before I went into this thing, I could never understand people who struggled with depression. I always wondered why they didn't just "snap out of it." Now I understand that depression is a normal part of life. And I have a lot more understanding when someone tells me that they are slugging through it.

This depression of mine ended up lasting two and a half years. And when it hit, I had no clue how to get out of it. I was completely confused and embarrassed. There were times when I wondered if I would *ever* come out of it.

That's when I began to study depression. And I began to notice how many of God's choice men had dealt with depression. Guys like Moses, David, Elijah, Jeremiah, Paul, along with a whole slew of others. Depression is one of the more subtle ambushes of the enemy. And the truth is that most men, at one time or another in their lives, are going to take a walk through some valley of depression. It is well known that Winston Churchill had many bouts with this affliction. He called it "the big, black dog."

There's a lot I could say here about depression, but I want to underline one thing. One of the ways you get through a depression and come out stronger on the other side is by having a good friend. Centuries ago someone pointed out that friendship doubles our joy and divides our grief. I found that out firsthand. In the course of my two-year battle with depression, God gave me several invaluable friends.

One of those friends was a guy named Sunny Arnold. Sunny had been through his own depression a number of years before—only to come out the other side stronger and wiser (see 2 Corinthians 1:3–5). He came alongside to provide a hindsight perspective when I was completely lacking in perspective. I owe Sunny big time.

Hank Raehn was another such friend. Hank and I met for lunch every other Friday over those two years. Hank had a way of listening and quietly sharing the burden. I never went away from a lunch with this faithful friend without a major dose of encouragement.

Another friend was my brother Jeff. On a moment's notice, he would take an hour or two out of his busy schedule so that we could talk. If he did that once, he did it fifty times. My brother Mike did the same thing. So did Mom and Dad, and my wife, Mary, was absolutely unbelievable. I'm very fortunate that my family is made up of friends. And in our family, when one of us gets in trouble, we immediately circle the wagons. Henry Drummond was right: "The family circle is the supreme conductor of Christianity."

Friends can show up in places you'd never expect. Even in a depression. And throughout that period, God graciously brought along all sorts of friends who encouraged me daily in their own unique ways.

The enemy loves to isolate us. He loves to get us alone. He loves to get us into that John Wayne, strong-silent-type, "I don't need anybody" mentality. That's not masculine. That's stupid.

The truth is that you and I desperately need a few good friends. Friends with whom we can share failure as well as success. Friends who are there when times are good and when times are bad. Friends who care about us enough to tell us when we're on track and when we're screwing up. If you've got a friend or two like that, your chances of finishing strong will go up a thousand percent!

Samuel Johnson exuded great wisdom with these words: "If a man does not make new acquaintances as he advances through life, he will soon find himself alone. A man, sir, must keep his friendships in constant repair."

Maybe you have a friendship that has grown a little distant. Why don't you call your friend up and take him to lunch? Do a little friendship repair. All you probably need to do is to change the oil. Or replace a few points and plugs.

Whatever it needs, fix it. And if he doesn't want to fix it, then move on to someone who is willing to be a friend. There's an old Scottish proverb that says, "He who ceases to be your friend never was a good one."

And one more thing. Start with your wife. If you don't maintain any other friendship, maintain that one. She knows you like a book—or at least, she should. Perhaps you need to take off the tinfoil and let her see your heart. All of it. A woman who is allowed to see inside her husband's heart is a woman who will become a friend for life.

STAY AWAY... FROM OTHER WOMEN

Though we've already touched on this in the previous chapter, it bears repeating: Keep your distance from other women.

I'm *not* saying that you become rude to women or stand-offish. I'm *not* saying that you gain a reputation for being discourteous, disrespectful, cold, or abrupt.

What I am saying is that we keep an *appropriate distance* in our relationships with the women with whom we work and associate. You don't need to be weird or act strange. You don't need to make anyone feel uncomfortable to be around you. But both the women that you work with and your wife will intuitively know by your behavior and actions that here is a man who is clean and pure in relationships with all women. Here's a man willing to go the extra mile in commitment to his wife.

We must keep our distance emotionally, and we must keep our distance physically. And if we do that, we'll be just fine.

One of the reasons the vast majority of guys don't finish strong can be found right here. Why don't they finish strong? Because the enemy takes them out. Satan's all-time, Numero Uno, time-proven tactic for snaring men and keeping them from finishing strong is sexual immorality. And the statistics prove it.

A recent, carefully controlled study of nearly thirty-five hundred men and women provided some insight to the thinking of a number of conservative Christian men. The findings were shockingly eye-opening.

Researchers divided respondents into three categories of attitudes toward sex: traditional, relational, and recreational. The *traditional* group said that religious belief always guides their sexual behavior and that premarital, extramarital, and homosexual sex is wrong. The *relational* group believed sex should be a part of a loving relationship but should not necessarily be restricted to marriage. The final group, the *recreational* proponents, believed sex should be enjoyed for its own sake and didn't necessarily have anything to do with love.[6]

Now here's the bombshell. Only 50.5 percent of conservative Protestants fall into the traditional category. *That means that half of evangelical Christians believe that sex does not necessarily have to be restricted to marriage.* Excuse me for saying so, but that's a crock. And according to the stats, one out of every two men who claim to be Christians buys that line. Can you believe that? Unfortunately, I think it's right on target.

I remember having a lunch conversation several years ago with a very successful, married, thirty-something guy who was an active member of a very solid evangelical church in his city. He had just read my book *Point Man* and posed this question to me: "Why did you spend at least one hundred pages of your book discussing sexual temptation?" He asked the question as though it were just a passing curiosity to him.

"Because I think sexual temptation is the number one issue in the lives of most men, and I think it's the primary way that the enemy picks off Christian men," I replied.

"Do you really believe it's that serious a problem?" he asked.

"Yes, I do. I think it's epidemic."

I got the distinct impression he found that hard to believe.

Six months later, a prominent married woman in that church turned up pregnant by the man who had asked me that question. And it wasn't his wife. She was some other guy's wife.

You may think this man is the exception. I think it would be safer to say that he is part of a "theologically conservative" group of Christians whose behavior has absolutely no relationship to their doctrinal beliefs.

The same study looked at the area of sexual faithfulness within marriage. Of those groups reporting only one sex partner in the last twelve months, those of the Jewish faith led all others. *Conservative Protestants came in second to last*, just slightly ahead of those who claimed no religious affiliation at all.[7]

In regard to pornography, *41 percent* of all men reported having done one of the following in the last twelve months: watching an X-rated movie, visiting a club with semi-nude or nude dancers, purchasing sexually explicit books, magazines, erotic devices or sex toys, or calling a sex phone number.[8]

But of course, those statistics have no relationship to Christians who believe in the authority of the Bible, are pro-life, and are committed to their families, right? Think again. A number of years ago a national conference for church youth directors was held at a major hotel in a city in the Midwest. Youth pastors by the hundreds flooded into that hotel and took nearly every room. At the conclusion of the conference, the hotel manager told the conference administrator that the number of guests who tuned into the adult movie channel broke the previous record, far and away outdoing any other convention in the history of the hotel.

Dr. Arch Hart works with a number of pastors across the country. And Hart believes that every person has his price. What he means is that, given the right person in the right circumstances, we all have the potential of paying the wrong price for a moment of pleasure. Dr. Hart goes on to model the principle of gut-level honesty with this personal comment:

> Early in our marriage I discovered what sort of person was *my* price: a
> woman with a particular appearance and personality. My wife could
> see it on my face when I was around someone like that. My wife has
> helped me be honest, to say, "That's a person who, for me, is so

attractive, I can't help myself," and then to take steps to avoid any problem.

A number of years ago I was driving home from the church office. I had spent the afternoon in counseling sessions. As I was driving home, I suddenly realized something about the woman I had just met with for the third time. I realized that, if I were a single man and were introduced to her, I would probably ask her out. But I was not single. I was married. And I wanted to stay married to the woman I loved very much.

So here's what I did. I went home and told my wife what I had realized. She knew this woman. And then I told Mary that I thought it would be best for me not to counsel with that woman again. This is also when I came up with my own personal policy of counseling a woman only once and then referring her. Now why did I decide to refer that woman to another person for counseling?

Did anything wrong happen in that session? No. Was anything said or done that was inappropriate? No. Did I question the motives of the woman who had come in for counseling? Absolutely not. She was genuinely trying to get some advice on her marriage. So why did I never meet with her again? Because some things are more important than life itself. Like removing myself from situations where I could possibly be tempted. Like taking steps to protect my relationship with my wife. Oh, yeah, and there's one other reason I no longer would continue that counseling situation. I want to finish strong.

Ministry begins at home. My first ministry responsibility is to my wife. My second is to my kids. So let me ask you a question. If you get tied up with some woman who isn't your wife, what kind of ministry are you going to have to your wife and kids? You won't. And if you don't have a ministry to your wife and kids, then, quite frankly, you are not going to finish strong.

As we will see in the next chapter, if you want to finish strong, there is one non-negotiable trait that you must embrace in your life regarding sexual temptation. And that trait is gut-level honesty.

STAY ALERT ... TO THE TACTICS OF THE ENEMY

If you're going to finish strong, you can't go through life on cruise control. You must *stay alert* to the schemes of the enemy. We are at war. And our foe is smarter and wiser than we are. David Roper has done a masterful job of describing our adversary:

> Satan is a gentleman, Bacon told us. A charming fellow with immense power, subtlety, and thousands of years of experience. His chief aim, of course, is to injure the God against whom he once rebelled. To accomplish this, Satan misrepresents the Creator to his creatures, always attempting to frustrate his good purposes for them and hopefully—in the process—break the heart of God. Satan promises us the world, but as Milton said, "All is false and hollow; though his tongue drops manna and makes the worse appear a better reason."9

What a great line! Satan makes the worse appear a *better* reason. Every guy who has ever been conned by the enemy has fallen for that line of reasoning.

- It really won't hurt anyone to sleep with this woman.
- Getting this divorce really won't hurt my kids. (Kids are resilient, aren't they?)
- Everybody fudges somewhere on their taxes.

That's making the worse appear to be a better reason. And falling for it will keep you from finishing strong. We are in a battle, my friend, and the stakes are unimaginably high.

Listen to the wise words of Martyn Lloyd-Jones:

> Not to realize that you are in a conflict means one thing only, and it is that you are so hopelessly defeated, and so "knocked out" as it were, that you do not even know it—you are unconscious! It means that you are completely defeated by the devil. Anyone who is not aware of

a fight and a conflict in a spiritual sense is in a drugged and hazardous condition.[10]

This is no time to be on sedatives. This is the time to stay alert! Too many men who have started well have failed to finish strong. History is strewn with the wreckage of their lives.

God give us men. A time like this demands

Strong minds, great hearts, true faith and ready hands.

Men whom the lust of office does not kill,

Men whom the spoils of office cannot buy,

Men who possess opinions and a will,

Men who love honor, men who will not lie.

—Josiah Gilbert Holland

Is that the kind of guy you want to be?

Then make sure you are stayed upon Jehovah.

Make sure you stay in…the Scriptures.

Make sure you stay close…to a friend.

Make sure you stay away…from other women.

Make sure you stay alert…to the tactics of the enemy.

That's how you can *anticipate* and *avoid* the ambushes. And if you're looking for a place to start, you only need to remember one thing.

Just a pinch between your cheek and gum.

PART TWO

THE PERILS TO FINISHING STRONG

CHAPTER FOUR

DRY SHIPWRECK

Kings ought to shear, not skin, their sheep.

ROBERT HERRICK

In the late 1800s, a distinguished member of the British Parliament traveled to Scotland to give a speech. On the way, his carriage became hopelessly mired in the thick mud of a rural road. A young Scottish farm boy suddenly appeared on the scene with a team of large draft horses. He quickly had the carriage out of its dilemma and ready to resume the journey.

The gentleman insisted on paying the young man, but the lad refused. He was simply being a good neighbor—and neighbors help each other out when there is difficulty.

The English lawmaker was immediately taken with the young man and his attitude.

"Are you sure I can't pay you for your time and effort?" the gentlemen asked.

"Thank you, sir, but it was the least that I could do. It was a privilege to help such an important person as yourself," the boy replied.

"What do you want to be when you grow up?" asked the man.

"I'd like to be a doctor, but I doubt that it will happen since my family does not have the money for such education."

"Then I will help you become a doctor," said the politician.

And as the years went by, the member of Parliament kept his promise.

Nearly fifty years later, another famous English statesman lay dangerously close to death due to pneumonia. Winston Churchill had become ill while attending a wartime conference, and England desperately needed his leadership as Hitler threatened to destroy their nation.

Churchill miraculously recovered because his physician gave him an injection of a new wonder drug called penicillin. Penicillin had recently been discovered by the brilliant medical doctor, Alexander Fleming.

Alexander Fleming was the young boy who had pulled the stalled carriage from the mud. And the man who promised to return the favor by sending him to medical school was Winston Churchill's father, Sir Randolph Churchill.

Randolph Churchill saw what no one else had seen in the face of that young Scottish farm boy. He saw potential. And his commitment to helping that young man reach his potential saved the life of his own son nearly half a century later. And by saving the life of Winston Churchill, indeed, he may have saved all of England.

Nobody knew Alexander Fleming as he worked in obscurity with the horses on his father's farm in Scotland. And no one knew David as he cared for his father's sheep in the secluded hills outside of Bethlehem.

As Alexander Fleming's life was changed forever in one day by meeting one great man, so David's life was changed forever when he met Samuel, the great prophet of Israel. Samuel saw in David what no one else saw. He not only saw potential, but he saw the future king of Israel.

But even Samuel might have missed that moment of recognition if the Lord had not whispered urgently in his heart's ear: "Arise, anoint him; for this is he" (1 Samuel 16:12). So Samuel anointed the young man on the spot, in the presence of his astonished family. And even then, it wasn't until years later that they began to see the greatness in the youngest son of Jesse.

In the early years of his youth, David was obscure. He was also unappreciated by his own father. When Samuel came to the house of Jesse, he came with the purpose of anointing one of Jesse's sons to become the next king. God had chosen one of these boys to succeed Saul. When Samuel saw David's older brother, Eliab, he thought he'd found his man. But God said no. As Samuel looked at the rest of the seven older sons of Jesse, none of them rang true. Samuel asked Jesse, "Are these all of your sons?"

Jesse replied that they were, except for his youngest son, David, who was out minding the sheep. They brought him in and the rest is history. David was God's choice to be king. And David's own father hadn't regarded him highly enough to include him in the meeting with the visiting prophet. It's always a tragedy when a father overlooks the potential in his own son. Jesse was raising the future king of Israel under his own roof, but he didn't have the vision to see it.

Do you have a son? Whatever you do, don't make Jesse's mistake. God will choose leaders for the next generation. And that great leader of the next generation may be running around your house right now with a diaper that needs changing and a nose that needs wiping. So make sure you take good care of the kid.

A FAST STARTER

Give David credit. He came out of the starting blocks like a greyhound after a rabbit. Months later, with the oil of Samuel's flask figuratively still flowing down from his head, David went directly to the battlefield to deliver some cheese sandwiches to his older brothers who were serving in Saul's army. That's when he found out that all of Israel was intimidated by this Philistine giant who went by the name of Goliath. And you know what followed.

David had a phenomenal start. If there were ever a surefire candidate to finish strong, it was David. If you were a betting man, David seemed a sure thing to finish "in the money."

"In the first ten chapters of 2 Samuel, David could do no wrong. He is never defeated in battle. Never wrong in judgment. He begins his reign in prayer and continues in faith. Enemies are subdued, the nation is unified, the capital secured, and the boundary extends from six thousand to sixty thousand square miles.

"But that is the first ten chapters."[1]

In chapter eleven, David shipwrecked. And his life would never be quite the same again. Before the shipwreck with Bathsheba, all David knew was triumph. After, all he knew was heartbreak and trouble.

Mark Twain knew the Mississippi River like a contentious sibling. A former riverboat captain, he was all too aware of the distinctive dangers of this massive river:

> Clear-water rivers with gravel bottoms change their channels very gradually, and therefore one needs to learn them but once; but piloting becomes another matter when you apply it to vast streams like the Mississippi and the Missouri, whose alluvial banks cave and change constantly, whose snags are always hunting up new quarters, whose sandbars are never at rest, whose channels are forever dodging and shirking, and whose obstructions must be confronted in all nights and all weathers without the aid of a single lighthouse or buoy; for there is neither light nor buoy to be found anywhere in all this three or four thousand miles of villainous river.[2]

There is an old Greek proverb that says, "The pilot of a ship is worth as much as all the crew." No crew member of a riverboat on the Mississippi would ever argue with that proverb. Every time a riverboat captain set out for another journey from St. Louis to Natchez, he was navigating a different river on the same stretch of water he'd traveled just two weeks prior. It wasn't unusual on the great river to pass the broken timbers of a riverboat that hadn't made the necessary course corrections. That's why the challenge of each voyage was always the same: finish strong.

Over the years there have been some monumental shipwrecks. We all know the great tragedy of the *Titanic* and the fascinating tale of Robinson Crusoe. Fact and fiction, poetry and song have woven around the theme of shipwrecks for hundreds of years. Some of it is truth, some of it is legend, and believe it or not, some of it is biblical (read about Paul's dramatic shipwreck in Acts 27–28).

In nautical history, there are three inescapable consequences to being shipwrecked that are true whether it's inland on the Mississippi or out on the open sea:

- Shipwrecks can take you farther than you wanted to go.

- Shipwrecks can keep you longer than you wanted to stay.

- Shipwrecks can cost you more than you wanted to pay.

That's exactly what happened to David. David shipwrecked. And that's precisely why David didn't finish strong. But there is something quite extraordinary about David's personal shipwreck. When David shipwrecked, he never got wet. David experienced a *dry* shipwreck. And in many ways, the dry shipwrecks are the most devastating shipwrecks of all.

So if David never got wet, then how did he actually shipwreck?

The answer is very clear in Scripture. David shipwrecked by watching *someone else* get wet:

> Then it happened in the spring, at the time when kings go out to
> battle, that David sent Joab and his servants with him and all Israel,
> and they destroyed the sons of Ammon and besieged Rabbah. But
> David stayed at Jerusalem.
>
> Now when evening came David arose from his bed and walked
> around on the roof of the king's house, and from the roof he saw a
> woman bathing; and the woman was very beautiful in appearance.
> (2 Samuel 11:1–2)

As a young man, David was off to an incredible start. But somewhere in his forties, David shipwrecked.

So David sent and inquired about the woman. And one said, "Is this not Bathsheba, the daughter of Eliam, the wife of Uriah the Hittite?" And David sent messengers and took her, and when she came to him, he lay with her; and when she had purified herself from her uncleanness, she returned to her house. And the woman conceived; and she sent and told David, and said, "I am pregnant." (2 Samuel 11:3–5)

Sin can shipwreck your life.

Throughout the Bible, there are three inescapable principles concerning sin. Just like shipwrecks,

- sin will take you farther than you wanted to go;
- sin will keep you longer than you wanted to stay;
- sin will cost you more than you wanted to pay.

A TITANIC MISTAKE

The plight of the *Titanic* may be the most famous shipwreck in all of history.

The sin of David with Bathsheba may be the most famous moral shipwreck in all of history.

And they have something extremely significant in common.

On April 10, 1912, the ship *Titanic* embarked on her maiden cruise from Southampton to New York. The ship was so carefully structured and engineered that it was billed as "the ship that God couldn't sink." (Oh yeah?) She was four city blocks long and carried the most up-to-date safety devices. She featured a French sidewalk cafe and luxurious suites…but she carried only twenty lifeboats for the 2200 passengers on board.

This great ship, whose size was greater than any other, whose integrity of construction and whose engines and equipment were the best that money could buy, sailed the seas for only five days. Despite her grand send-off, she hit an iceberg and sank in just two hours and forty minutes. A total of 1523 people lost their lives in the greatest shipwreck of modern history. Only 705 survivors were picked up from her half-filled lifeboats.

But the *Titanic* shipwrecked days before she ever hit the iceberg. How could the greatest ocean liner ever built shipwreck hours *before* she hit the iceberg? The *Titanic* sealed her own fate because she failed to heed the repeated warnings of imminent danger.

For almost her entire voyage, *Titanic* had been advised repeatedly of ice conditions at or near the position her sailing orders required her to occupy. Throughout the day of April 14, as she approached this location, her wireless operators received at least six messages which described field ice and icebergs on her course directly ahead.

One message (from the ship *Athinai* via the ship *Baltic*) was not posted until more than five hours after it had been received. Another message (at 7:30 P.M., *Californian* to *Antillian*) was not shown to the captain, since to do so would interrupt his dinner. Yet another message (from *Mesaba*) was never taken to the bridge as the wireless operator was working alone and could not leave his equipment. The receipt of a final, crucial message (from *Californian*) was interrupted and never completed when *Titanic's* operator impatiently cut it off so that he might continue his own commercial traffic.

There had even been a visual warning at 10:30 P.M. from the *Rappahannock*, whose Morse lamp message about the heavy field ice directly ahead was briefly acknowledged from the *Titanic's* bridge. There is no evidence that this vital information was ever heeded; nor was it ever given to Captain Smith, now dozing in his quarters.[3]

In actuality, the *Titanic* shipwrecked before it ever hit that iceberg. And so did David. David shipwrecked morally years before he ever saw Bathsheba stepping into the bathwater.

David set the course for his own shipwreck the moment he married a second wife. Then he married a third. By that time he was on a roll, and he married a fourth, followed by a fifth, and by the time he was thirty, he had six wives.

David was a polygamist. That word means "many marriages" or "many-wived." God's plan for David was that he be a "one-woman kind of man." But David wanted to be a "many-wived kind of man." And by doing so, he engineered his own personal shipwreck.

Most people didn't realize what was happening to David. They had no idea he was taking on water and riding lower and lower in the waves. After all, the kings of the surrounding nations all had multiple wives. But Israel was not to be like the other nations, and David was not to take his cues from other kings. And in his gut, he knew it. But he wouldn't heed the warnings that inevitably came from the Spirit of God. He refused to change his course.

For just as the *Titanic* failed to heed the six warnings, so David failed to heed at least six warnings. Every time he considered taking an additional wife, I firmly believe the Holy Spirit would send a telegram to his conscience. And just as the *Titanic* ignored the warnings, so did David.

Do you know the greatest tragedy of both shipwrecks? Both of them could have been *easily* avoided. But they weren't. And the world will continue to speak of both for centuries to come.

A DIRECT ORDER

In the book of Deuteronomy, God laid down a direct order to His people:

> "When you enter the land which the LORD your God gives you, and
> you possess it and live in it, and you say, 'I will set a king over me like
> all the nations who are around me,' you shall surely set a king over
> you whom the LORD your God chooses, one from among your
> countrymen you shall set as king over yourselves; you may not put a
> foreigner over yourselves who is not your countryman. Moreover, he
> shall not multiply horses for himself, nor shall he cause the people to
> return to Egypt to multiply horses, since the LORD has said to you, 'You
> shall never again return that way.' Neither shall he multiply wives for

himself, lest his heart turn away; nor shall he greatly increase silver and gold for himself." (Deuteronomy 17:14–17)

Now track closely with me here, because there is a critical lesson in all this for those of us who want to finish strong. God made it very clear that any king of Israel was not to multiply horses or multiply wives. And David clearly understood both directives.

Why didn't God want the king of Israel to multiply horses? What's the big deal about having a few more horses? Horses were used for warfare, and God didn't want Israel using horses in battle. He didn't want Israel to trust in their vast numbers of horses when they went to war; He wanted Israel to trust in Him. When David was king, he was careful to obey God's command about multiplying horses. An example of this is in 1 Chronicles 19. In this account, a huge military coalition of thirty-two thousand soldiers—along with numerous horses and chariots—gathered to war against Israel.

Against that mighty cavalry and countless armored chariots, David sent in his foot soldiers. And against all odds, Israel was victorious. Why were they victorious when they didn't send in any chariots and horses? They were victorious because they trusted in the Lord. David was very careful to follow this part of the command from Deuteronomy 17:16. How well did he have that concept down? He even celebrated it in one of his victory psalms!

Some trust in chariots and some in horses,
but we trust in the name of the LORD our God. (Psalm 20:7, NIV)

Yet there was a *second* part of the command in Deuteronomy 17 that David also must have known…but chose to ignore. David had an easier time with horses, it seems, than he had with women. And this became the basis for his shipwreck.

Somewhere around the age of eighteen, give or take a year or two, David was anointed by Samuel to be king of Israel. David did not actually become king until he was thirty. When David was anointed to become king at eighteen, he had no wife. When he assumed the throne at thirty, he had six wives.

F. B. Meyer sums up what happened to David before he ever shipwrecked with Bathsheba: "In direct violation of the law of Moses, he took more concubines and wives; fostering in him a habit of sensual indulgence, which predisposed him to the evil invitation of that evening hour."[4]

David's first wife was Michal, the daughter of Saul. When David was on the run from Saul in his twenties, Saul took Michal and married her to another man. David then married Ahinoam. After this second marriage, there is no doubt that David was clearly in sin every time he took another wife.

David eventually had *eight* wives. Some scholars think he had as many as twelve. There is no Susan, Linda, Donna, or Cathy in this group of wives. Try these names on for size: Michal, Ahinoam, Abigail (that's the only normal one in the bunch), Maacah, Haggith, Ablital, Eglah, and Bathsheba. In addition to these eight wives who are named, he had at least ten concubines! By these eight wives, David had twenty-one sons and one daughter. And he had even more children by his concubines. To put it plainly, by ignoring God's command to be a one-woman man, David had one, very large, messed-up family. And he would live to regret it.

Polygamy was the continual crack in David's armor. And he passed it on to his son Solomon. Many sons attempt to outdo their fathers. Solomon was no exception. Following the example set by his father, Solomon accrued seven hundred wives and three hundred concubines. And Scripture writes the tragic epitaph of Solomon's life: "and his wives turned his heart away" (1 Kings 11:3). That's almost the precise wording of God's original warning in Deuteronomy 17. Kind of scary, isn't it? God's Word has a way of proving itself literally true—not only the "blessing" parts we like so much, but also the "warning" parts we don't always like so much.

Solomon was the son of a man known as "a man after His [God's] own heart." But the crack in the armor of David became the gaping hole in the fortress wall of Solomon's heart and eventually turned his heart away from the Lord.

Let me ask you a question. Are there any other wives in your life? It's amazing how many Christian guys have more than one wife. Does that surprise you? It shouldn't. Unfortunately, it happens all the time.

It's not uncommon to meet a Christian man who is polygamous. His first wife is Sarah, his second is pornography, his third is soft porn movies when he's traveling, and his fourth is calling sexually explicit 900 numbers.

We don't think of those activities as "other wives," but that's what they are. Kings would collect wives like toys. And it's still happening thousands of years later.

You see, David couldn't buy a pornographic magazine or watch a late-night, soft porn movie on HBO or Showtime. So in order to get some sexual kicks, he would marry another wife. That was David's centerfold. Today you don't have to marry another woman to get illicit sexual thrills. These "other women" are waiting in full-color magazines, in videos, and on cable. You can even download them off the Internet.

So once again, I pose the question. Are you a polygamist? Maybe you've never thought that pornography makes you a "many-wived man." But it does. And there's one more thing about these other wives. Just like David's multiple wives, these wives of the 1990s also bear children.

If you marry the other wife of pornography, she will bear you a child by the name of "Shame."

If you marry the other wife of HBO soft porn movies, she will bear you a child called "Guilt."

If you marry the other wife of prostitution, she will bear you the child of "Humiliation."

If you don't believe that, then take a hard look at the disgraced evangelists of the '80s.

My friend, you don't need another "wife" and you don't need any more "children." At least not *those* kinds of children. But if you don't put away these other wives now, then you should know that you are on the same exact course that both the *Titanic* and David charted.

But you should also know it's not too late to change course! You don't have to keep bearing toward those killer icebergs. There is plenty of open sea. It's not too late to hit "all stop" or "left full rudder" and *get outta there*. There is absolutely no reason in the world for you to keep steaming along in the wrong direction. Unless you are bullheaded. Or just plain stupid.

You don't *have* to shipwreck.

Get rid of that other wife. Today. Call your pastor and tell him what's been going on. Or if you have a buddy you can trust, call him. You need to confess that sin, not only to the Lord, but also to a friend you can count on. James put it this way, "Confess your sins to one another, and pray for one another, so that you may be healed." Healed of what? Healed of your lust for the other wives that are eating your lunch.

Remember...

- Sin will take you farther than you wanted to go.
- Sin will keep you longer than you wanted to stay.
- Sin will cost you more than you wanted to pay.

Let's consider those thoughts in just a little more detail.

SIN WILL TAKE YOU FARTHER THAN YOU WANTED TO GO

Captain Edward J. Smith was given the honor of command for *Titanic's* maiden voyage. The gleaming new liner was part of the prestigious White Star Fleet. Captain Smith, fifty-nine years old, was senior commander of the fleet and was always given command of a ship's maiden voyage.

Captain Smith had planned that the *Titanic's* first voyage would be his last. After he got the ship to New York, he was going to retire. At the age of fifty-nine, he was in good health and he still had many things he wanted to accomplish. Captain Smith only wanted to go as far as New York. Due to the shipwreck, he went farther than he wanted to go. About thirteen thousand feet farther. In the wrong direction.

During her single, interrupted voyage one element of misjudgment
was added to another in a deadly chain. Warnings went unheeded.
Errors in safety standards and navigations were combined to generate
the inevitable tragic conclusion.[5]

Captain Smith had been headed for retirement. He wound up in an icy
coffin thousands of feet below the sea lanes he had traversed so often. Shipwrecks will take you farther than you wanted to go.

When David stood on his roof in the balmy twilight, watching the beautiful Bathsheba step out of her clothes, the only thing on his mind was to enjoy
her charms firsthand. That was about as far as he wanted to go. But sin will take
you *farther* than you wanted to go. David had only planned on a discreet
evening of adultery, yet within weeks he was guilty of betrayal, murder, and a
heinous cover-up. And that was a winding road he'd never planned to travel.

David was shrewd. Give him that much. When Bathsheba turned up pregnant, David immediately sent to the battlefield for her husband, Uriah. This
would cover his bases and no one would ever be the wiser. David made the classic mistake that men have been making for thousands of years: he thought that
he could use deception to cover disobedience. But that's not how it works.
Deception *never* covers disobedience. It just makes it worse. Count on it, your
sin *will* find you out. And it will take you farther than you wanted to go.

Then David sent to Joab, saying, "Send me Uriah the Hittite." So Joab
sent Uriah to David. When Uriah came to him, David asked
concerning the welfare of Joab and the people and the state of the war.
Then David said to Uriah, "Go down to your house, and wash your
feet." And Uriah went out of the king's house, and a present from the
king was sent out after him. But Uriah slept at the door of the king's
house with all the servants of his lord, and did not go down to his
house. Now when they told David, saying, "Uriah did not go down to
his house," David said to Uriah, "Have you not come from a journey?

Why did you not go down to your house?" And Uriah said to David,
"The ark and Israel and Judah are staying in temporary shelters, and
my lord Joab and the servants of my lord are camping in the open
field. Shall I then go to my house to eat and to drink and to lie with
my wife? By your life and the life of your soul, I will not do this thing."
Then David said to Uriah, "Stay here today also, and tomorrow I will
let you go." So Uriah remained in Jerusalem that day and the next.
Now David called him, and he ate and drank before him, and he made
him drunk; and in the evening he went out to lie on his bed with his
lord's servants, but he did not go down to his house.

Now it came about in the morning that David wrote a letter to
Joab, and sent it by the hand of Uriah. And he had written in the letter,
saying, "Place Uriah in the front line of the fiercest battle and withdraw
from him, so that he may be struck down and die." (2 Samuel 11:6–15)

And that's exactly what Joab did.

David had been driving fast for a long time on the freeway of sexual grati-
fication. He only planned to go as far as the exit marked "Adultery." But the
momentum of his deceit took him all the way to the off-ramp of "Murder." In
David's mind, "there was no alternative but that [Uriah] should die, for dead
men tell no tales. If a child were to be born, Uriah's lips, at least, should not be
able to disown it."[6]

I believe it was Goethe who once said, "To act is easy, to think is hard."
David acted but he didn't think. If he had thought about it, he would have realized that deceit could not cover his disobedience. But he didn't think. And it
took him farther than he wanted to go.

I don't know what's going on in your life, and you don't know what's going
on in mine. But I can tell you this. If either one of us is playing around with
hidden sin, it's eventually going to come out. You've got an accelerator and
you've got a brake. When it comes to sin, you need to hit the brake. Stop NOW.

Put on a bumper sticker that says, "I Brake for Hidden Sin." If you don't, you're going to find yourself a lot farther down the road of destruction than you ever planned on going. And it's tough—so agonizingly tough—to come back.

SIN WILL KEEP YOU LONGER THAN YOU WANTED TO STAY

"Women and children first!"

Captain Smith's stern order echoed across the ship when the seriousness of the situation on board became apparent. But many wives didn't want to leave their husbands.

Mr. and Mrs. Lucien Smith were arguing when Mrs. Smith went directly to the captain. She explained to the captain that her husband was all she had in the world and that she couldn't live without him. The captain ignored her pleas and once again shouted into his megaphone, "Women and children first!"

Mr. Smith then took his wife in his arms and said, "I never expected to ask you to obey me, but this is one time that you must. It is only a matter of form to have women and children go first. This ship is thoroughly equipped and everyone on her will be saved."

With that assurance, Mrs. Smith got into the boat. She never saw her husband again. Shipwrecks can keep you longer than you intended to stay.

There were many notable passengers on the *Titanic*. Perhaps the best known was John Jacob Astor. In 1918, he had a personal fortune estimated at somewhere between seventy-five and one hundred million dollars. Astor was forty-eight years old and his wife, Madeleine, was just nineteen—and five-months pregnant. Astor assisted his wife into the boat and assured her he would soon follow in another. Legend has it that he quipped, "I asked for ice, but this is ridiculous." He then went to the kennel to get his pet Airedale, Kitty, so she could accompany him. Both of them went down with the *Titanic*.

The passengers of the *Titanic* had been deceived into believing that every possible safety measure had been taken. As a result, over fifteen hundred were kept longer than they wanted to stay.

Adam Clarke was a sales clerk in a store that sold fine silk to people of the upper classes in London. One day his employer showed young Adam how he could increase sales and profits by subtly stretching the silk as he measured it out.

Young Adam Clarke looked his employer straight in the eye and said, "Sir, your silk may stretch but my conscience won't."

By the time David had sinned with Bathsheba, he had been stretching his conscience for years. Even after his adulterous act and the murder of Uriah, David continued to act as though everything was just fine and dandy. But it wasn't. David kept showing up for religious services on Sunday morning, Sunday night, and even Wednesday night. He may have been in a small group Bible study. But he was living a lie. He was covering up adultery and murder.

About a year after the murder of Uriah, the prophet Nathan showed up and told David of a heartless crime that had been committed in his kingdom.

> Then the LORD sent Nathan to David. And he came to him, and said,
> "There were two men in one city, the one rich and the other poor. The
> rich man had a great many flocks and herds. But the poor man had
> nothing except one little ewe lamb which he bought and nourished;
> and it grew up together with him and his children. It would eat of his
> bread and drink of his cup and lie in his bosom, and was like a
> daughter to him. Now a traveler came to the rich man, and he was
> unwilling to take from his own flock or his own herd, to prepare for
> the wayfarer who had come to him; rather he took the poor man's ewe
> lamb and prepared it for the man who had come to him." Then
> David's anger burned greatly against the man, and he said to Nathan,
> "As the LORD lives, surely the man who has done this deserves to die.
> And he must make restitution for the lamb fourfold, because he did
> this thing and had no compassion."
> Nathan then said to David, "You are the man!" (2 Samuel 12:1–7)

The Word of God is like a mirror. And when Nathan had drawn the unwitting and indignant king completely into his little trap, the king suddenly recognized himself in the mirror. He had just passed judgment on himself. God had been trying to get his attention for twelve months, but David would not listen. Sin had kept him longer than he had planned to stay.

SIN WILL COST YOU MORE THAN YOU WANTED TO PAY

The passengers of the *Titanic* who booked first-class accommodations paid thousands of dollars to have the very best. Many of them were wealthy beyond the common man's wildest dreams. Yet this was a trip that cost every one of them more than they were willing to pay.

In the stateroom of Major Arthur Peuchen sat an ornate tin box that contained two hundred thousand dollars in bonds and one hundred thousand dollars in preferred stock. The major quickly changed out of his tuxedo into two pairs of long underwear and heavy clothes. Then, looking at the tin box, he impulsively grabbed three oranges, stuffed them into his pockets, and slammed the door of his room behind him, leaving the box behind. Shipwrecks have a way of costing you more than you wanted to pay.

David ultimately confessed and repented of his great sin. But there are painful consequences that follow even our confessed sin. *That's why we want to avoid sin in the first place.* David's sin with Bathsheba and the murder of Uriah cost him a huge price.

- It cost him dearly when his infant son died.
- It cost him dearly when his oldest son, Amnon, raped his half-sister and David's daughter, Tamar.
- It cost him dearly when his son Absalom killed his brother Amnon to avenge the rape of Tamar.
- It cost him dearly when years later, his trusted friend and counselor, Ahithophel, assisted young Absalom in a plot to overthrow David and rip the kingdom out of his hands.

Why would Ahithophel betray David whom he had served for decades? A fast look at the genealogical chart answers the question. Ahithophel was the grandfather of Bathsheba and the father of Eliam. Who was Eliam? Probably the best friend of Uriah. No wonder Ahithophel turned on David.

David was never the same after his adultery. Before his shipwreck with Bathsheba, David's life was characterized by *triumph*. After the shipwreck, there is only one word that describes the rest of David's life: *trouble*.

The next time some sin looks particularly attractive, remember the consequences of sin that haunted David for the rest of his life. Whatever that specific sin is, it's not worth it. You can take this to the bank: no matter how alluring the sin looks right now, it will wind up costing you more than you are willing to pay.

It's time to wrap up this chapter. But there's one critical point that needs to be made.

A case could be argued that David never fully repented of his polygamy. When you go to the end of his life and find him ready to die and in physical weakness, a young virgin was brought in to be David's companion and "to keep him warm."

> Now King David was old, advanced in age; and they covered him with clothes, but he could not keep warm. So his servants said to him, "Let them seek a young virgin for my lord the king, and let her attend the king and become his nurse; and let her lie in your bosom, that my lord the king may keep warm." So they searched for a beautiful girl throughout all the territory of Israel, and found Abishag the Shunammite, and brought her to the king. And the girl was very beautiful; and she became the king's nurse and served him, but the king did not cohabit with her. (1 Kings 1:1–4)

Why didn't David have one of his regular wives keep him warm? Obviously, Bathsheba had been able to keep him warm on more than one occasion. Why didn't he call for Bathsheba? David is simply repeating the same pattern that he chose all of his life. It was just another compromise. Even though there was no sexual contact with this young woman who was brought to him at the end of his life, the modus operandi is the same. When David had a need, he compromised and looked for someone new to meet his need.

David had compromised and compromised for so many years that he instinctively reverted back to it when he was near death and couldn't keep warm. Max Lucado said it best about David: "Mark it down. Compromise *chills* the soul."[7]

The iceberg that shipwrecked David was in his own heart. He allowed it free reign in his soul to drift unchecked on the sea of moral and sexual compromise. Tragically, it was the iceberg of a cold and compromising heart that brought him down.

I've got a question for you.

What's the temperature of your heart?

There is no more important question that you could ponder…if you want to finish strong.

CHAPTER FIVE

THE STATUS BROTHERS AND THEIR NOT-QUITE-RIGHT FIRST COUSIN, PRIDE

The greatest fault is to be
conscious of none.

THOMAS CARLYLE

You've probably heard of the Uzi.

But have you ever heard of Uzziah?

The Uzi is a famous machine gun made in Israel.

Uzziah was a king who ruled over Judah, the nation that used to be part of greater Israel before its civil war.

What the Uzi and Uzziah have in common is this: they were both capable of a strong burst.

Even though he lived three thousand years ago in the nation of Judah, Uzziah is a man who would fit very well into contemporary American culture. The reason he would fit so well is because he is a man who must be characterized as a successful man—and we live in a society intoxicated with success.

The media constantly barrages us with information and advertising that calls us to a "more successful lifestyle" than we currently enjoy. Just about everybody is trying to make his or her mark. Just about everybody wants to "get ahead." Just about everybody wants a bigger handful of "personal fulfillment.

FINISHING STRONG

I like this quote from Anthony Campolo so much I've used it a number of times:

> Success is a shining city. A pot of gold at the end of the rainbow. We
> dream of it as children. We strive for it through our adult lives, and we
> suffer melancholy at old age if we have not reached it. For success is
> the place of happiness, and the anxieties we suffer at the thought of
> not arriving there gives us ulcers, heart attacks, and nervous disorders.
> If our reach exceeds our grasp and we fail to achieve what we want,
> life seems meaningless and we feel emotionally dead in our culture.[1]

Why? Because success is at the forefront of our personal goals. Everybody wants to be "a success." Everybody wants his kids to be successful. But the world defines success in a different way than God's Word defines success. I think we need to make a clear distinction here, if we want to be men who finish strong. The world's call and the Bible's call are very different. In fact, they are diametrically opposed. What the world says about success is absolutely contrary to what Jesus Christ calls you and me to as His disciples.

SUCCESS: A DEFINITION

John Johnson has penned a definition of success that I think really nails what our world believes. "Success," he wrote, "is attaining cultural goals that are sure to elevate one's perceived importance in that culture."

Note that word "perceived." It doesn't *actually* elevate your importance, but it elevates your perceived importance. When people are successful (by the world's standards), they experience elevation in at least one of three areas: power, privilege, and wealth.

POWER

What do I mean by power? Having commands obeyed and wishes granted.

98

Back in the '80s I remember reading the autobiography of Lee Iacocca. During his years at Ford, he reflected on the fact that you always knew when you had "arrived" as a top executive. That is the day when you are handed a key to the executive washroom. Hey, it's just a key to a bathroom! But when you get that key, you've got a little more status, a little more clout. It's a sign of your enhanced power in the company. If you have a key to the executive washroom, you're used to having commands obeyed and wishes granted. People defer to you.

PRIVILEGE

Privilege means enjoying special rights or favors.

I like privilege, don't you? A number of years ago Mary and I checked into a hotel at about two in the morning. We were speaking at a conference and our plane had been delayed for six hours. When we finally arrived, they couldn't find our reservations. And the hotel was full. Finally the clerk said, "Mr. Farrar, we have a suite for you."

When he said "suite," I thought he meant "sweet." As in Hershey bar. And that would have been fine, too. But because of their mistake, they put us up in the only room left in the hotel. The Presidential Suite.

So we took the elevator up to the nosebleed floors in this big hotel and sauntered into "our suite." It was huge. Double doors. Large entryway. A couple of bedrooms with big TVs in each bedroom. A living room. A balcony. A phone in the bathroom, for goodness' sake. And an autographed picture of Ronald Reagan on the wall, thanking the hotel for such a wonderful visit. I mean, this really was a presidential suite!

I kind of liked that. I liked staying in a suite. I liked having a phone in the bathroom. I could get used to that real fast. I could get used to having a maid come in and turn down the covers for me and put two little mints on my pillow every night. That's nice. What was even better was that there were six beds in this suite and I got to walk around the place eating all the mints.

That's privilege.

If you're in a suite, you've got an elevation in status. You're not staying down there in the regular rooms with all those regular people. You're big time. It's a great feeling to be in a presidential suite. Especially when you're not paying for it.

WEALTH

Ah, we know about wealth, don't we? That's accumulating financial reserves and securities.

One credit company offers three cards, in three different colors. There's a Green Card, and it's a great little slab of plastic. You can buy all kinds of stuff with it and get into serious debt just as fast as you want to. This thing will take you from zero to fifteen hundred bucks in 3.5 seconds.

But then they have a Gold Card. This is just a shade more prestigious than the Green Card. It's a classy looking thing, and the ads on TV lead you to believe it's for those who are fiscally responsible and mature—or something like that. Once you've held a Gold Card, the Green Card looks kind of…ordinary.

But now they've come out with a Platinum Card, which makes the Gold Card users feel like second-class citizens. But it's interesting…as I've read about the Platinum Card, it really doesn't do much more than the other two. But I did find one major difference. The Green Card is $35 a year, the Gold Card is $65, and the Platinum is $250. Why would people want to shovel out that much money a year for a card like that? Because it makes them feel as though they've had an elevation in status.

When the world system talks about "success," it's talking about an elevation of status. Our culture is constantly giving us this information. And as Christians, we need to be careful that we're filtering this stuff through the grid of Scriptures, rather than buying it lock, stock, and Gold Card.

Yes, the ancient King Uzziah would have fit very nicely into our success-obsessed culture. If you were ever to meet this man, you couldn't help but be impressed by his aura of success. He enjoyed incredible power, privilege, and wealth. No doubt about it, he was a Platinum kind of guy.

U Z Z I A H ' S   R O O T S

You remember King David, and you probably remember his son Solomon. When Solomon died, the nation of Israel split into two kingdoms; they had a civil war just as America did in the 1800s. They ended up with a northern kingdom called Israel and a southern kingdom called Judah. Uzziah was the tenth guy on the throne in Judah after Solomon.

Second Chronicles 26 gives us a picture of some of this man's roots. Note verse one:

> And all the people of Judah took Uzziah, who was sixteen years old,
> and made him king in the place of his father Amaziah.

Verse three adds:

> Uzziah was sixteen years old when he became king, and he reigned
> fifty-two years in Jerusalem; and his mother's name was Jechiliah of
> Jerusalem.

His father had been king for six years. And after being king for six years, he elevated his teenaged son to serve with him, which they did for twenty-three years. Then his father died and he ruled alone for twenty-nine more years. He had a long, long reign as king of Judah.

Uzziah had a long race, and he was great out of the blocks. He had a fine start at this business of manhood and kinghood. Scripture puts it like this in verses four and five.

> And he did right in the sight of the LORD according to all that his father
> Amaziah had done. And he continued to seek God in the days of
> Zechariah, who had understanding through the vision of God; and as
> long as he sought the LORD, God prospered him.

This boy was unique—an unusual teenager. Here's a young man who had a heart for God early on in life. He sought God. He wanted a relationship with God. He talked to the Lord and did his best to live a life pleasing to the Lord.

We all know that the teenage years are difficult years because of incredibly intense peer pressure. As teenage kids, we are pressured and encouraged to "do what everybody else is doing," even if it violates the morals we learned at home.

But young Uzziah hung in there. He got off on the right foot and had his priorities set correctly from Day One. He was a very fortunate young man. Today he would have been a leader in the church high school group. He would have been sharing his faith. He would have been involved in discipleship. Uzziah was excited and energized by the God of his fathers. What incredible potential this teenager possessed!

Do you remember guys in your high school who seemed to have limitless potential? They were great athletes or gifted speakers. They hauled in good grades and dated all the right girls. They were guys who just stood out. They got their names in the yearbook as "Most Likely to Succeed." And you'd look at them and say, "Man, does that guy have potential."

Where were those guys by your ten-year reunion? How about your twenty-year reunion? Did they still have the world by the tail? Did they still seem like the cream on top of the bucket? You really don't know until all that "potential" gets put to the test in the real world, do you?

I've talked to guys who came back from their twenty-year reunions just shaking their heads. The kids everybody thought were going to conquer the world have kind of blended into the woodwork; there's nothing special about them. Besides that, they've gained weight and lost a lot of hair and don't look as awesome as they did in high school. When I went back to my twenty-year high school reunion, one of the first people I bumped into was one of the prom queens. She recognized me right away, despite my gray hair and the fact that I had gained a few pounds. But I had problems recognizing her. There was more to her than I remembered—quite a bit more.

But something else surprised me, too. A few of the biggest nerds in the class who couldn't seem to relate to anybody are millionaires now. They own software companies in Silicon Valley, wear Italian suits, and drive BMWs. I should be such a nerd.

Some guys who seem to have a lot of potential can't pull it off after they emerge from initial successes as a teenager. But Uzziah wasn't like that. He started off on the right foot and kept up the pace for a long time. He had a string of successes as an adult to match all that shining potential of his teenage years.

Second Chronicles 26 gives King Uzziah a very impressive résumé. Please take a minute to read it carefully.

> He built Eloth and restored it to Judah....
>
> Now he went out and warred against the Philistines, and broke down the wall of Gath and the wall of Jabneh and the wall of Ashdod; and he built cities in the area of Ashdod and among the Philistines. And God helped him against the Philistines, and against the Arabians who lived in Gur-baal, and the Meunites. The Ammonites also gave tribute to Uzziah, and his fame extended to the border of Egypt, for he became very strong. Moreover, Uzziah built towers in Jerusalem at the Corner Gate and at the Valley Gate and at the corner buttress and fortified them. And he built towers in the wilderness and hewed many cisterns, for he had much livestock, both in the lowland and in the plain. He also had plowmen and vinedressers in the hill country and the fertile fields, for he loved the soil. Moreover, Uzziah had an army ready for battle, which entered combat by divisions, according to the number of their muster, prepared by Jeiel the scribe and Maaseiah the official, under the direction of Hananiah, one of the king's officers. The total number of the heads of the households, of valiant warriors, was 2,600. And under their direction was an elite army of 307,500, who could wage war with great power, to help the king against the enemy. Moreover, Uzziah prepared for all the army shields, spears, helmets, body armor, bows and sling stones. And in Jerusalem he made engines of war invented by skillful men to be on the towers and on the corners, for the

purpose of shooting arrows and great stones. Hence his fame spread afar, for he was marvelously helped until he was strong. (vv. 2, 6–15)

Let's try to summarize some of this stuff. Verse two says he restored the key coastal city of Eloth, a strategic naval base and copper-smelting center of the day. Bringing that city on line was critical to the economic future of Judah, and Uzziah pulled it off.

Verse six tells us that he defeated major enemy cities. Lots of kings could claim that accomplishment, of course, but Uzziah was different. He defeated them and then turned around and rebuilt them. Did you ever hear of the Marshall Plan coming out of World War II? Uzziah had his own Marshall Plan, rebuilding captured cities and making them strong again. The Star of David rippled confidently in the breeze on flagpoles over cities that once were enemy strongholds.

Verses seven and eight remind us that he defeated some long-time enemies of his people—enemies who had been thorns in the side of Israel and Judah for generations.

Verse nine describes some of his building projects. The king oversaw some huge construction projects in the capital city. The man was a visionary and a builder.

Verse ten tells us he built fortresses outside of Jerusalem to protect his vast holdings of livestock. He also undertook vast agricultural projects to feed his people and make the nation of Judah self-sufficient. He was a planner and an administrator, a man who knew how to get things done.

Verses eleven and thirteen tell us that he reorganized Judah's military to make it more effective. He went after what might have been a bloated military bureaucracy. By the time he was finished trimming, cutting, and reorganizing, he had a powerful, efficient fighting force, equipped with the most advanced weapons and state-of-the-art technology.

How can you help but be impressed by a man of this caliber? You look at his life and you say, "This guy not only had potential, but he pulled it off." Today he would be called an entrepreneur…a super-achiever. You'd hear his name on the nightly business reports.

Is it surprising, then, to read the comment in verse fifteen?

> Hence his fame spread afar…

Sure, a king is famous just because he is king. That puts you in an elite class of world rulers. But this guy had more than a title; he was famous for what he *accomplished*. His name and fame spread far and wide. No other king of Israel or Judah—with the exception of Solomon—accomplished so much.

But verse fifteen is also what I consider to be a "hinge" verse in this story. It's certainly a hinge verse in the life of this man, Uzziah.

> Hence his fame spread afar, for he was marvelously helped until he
> was strong.

Do you note that word "until"?

It's a scary word. It means something is going to change. It's like when you're watching a movie, and suddenly the background music starts sounding a little tense, a little sinister. Something is going to be different. Life is moving along in one direction, and then something happens to move it in another direction. And then life changes, and nothing is ever the same again.

For lots of us, that word "until" had a good meaning at some point in our lives. We were barreling down an expressway to hell, living totally for ourselves, with no thought for God UNTIL…until we met the Lord Jesus Christ. He gave us a new heart, a new purpose, a new lease on life, and a new destination. That was a great "until." The best "until" there ever was.

But not all "untils" are good. Uzziah's wasn't. Remember, earlier in the chapter it said that this man "did right in the sight of the LORD" and that he "sought God during the days of Zechariah, who instructed him in the fear of God" (NIV).

Uzziah was God's man. He followed God's ways and pursued God's friendship. He was a student of the Word and learned at the feet of a great Bible teacher. So we get the feeling, as we read these verses, that everything he did had the stamp of God's approval on it. He ruled over Judah with the smile of the Lord over everything he did. What a great way to live! No wonder he was successful! As verse fifteen puts it, "he was marvelously helped." Another way to say that is "he was helped by a marvelous God who loved him."

Until.

Until something happened.

Until something changed.

Until he turned in another direction.

Until he chose to remove himself from God's protection and power.

And life was never the same after that.

In spite of all his achievements and history-making success, Uzziah reached a point where his spiritual life took a dramatic nosedive. He went into a spin, and to the best of our knowledge, he was never able to pull out of that spin. He started very strong and climbed very high...but he didn't finish strong. He screwed up. He crashed and burned. Here's what Scripture says:

> But when he became strong, his heart was so proud that he acted
> corruptly, and he was unfaithful to the LORD his God. (v. 16)

You know something? This verse scares me. And it ought to scare you, too. It's another one of those stories about a man who had everything in the world going for him but ended up throwing it all in the toilet and heading in another direction. It's like a kind of insanity that hits men in the middle part of life, and it makes me sweat to think about it.

What happened to this guy? How do things like this come about? How did Uzziah fly so far off course and get shot down over enemy territory?

As I read between the lines of Scripture, I think there are three possible answers. And don't leave these answers as part of ancient history. They are as up-to-date and relevant as this morning's *USA Today*.

THREE REASONS FOR UZZIAH'S FALL

Unless I miss my guess, I'd say the number one reason Uzziah ran into that terrible "until" was that *he began to spend more time and attention on the external rather than the eternal.*

Some have called this "the barrenness of a busy life." You know what it's like: we're trying to make it, we're trying to succeed. We're pouring our energies and our focus and our thoughts into getting ahead. And somehow we forget that true success has a lot more to do with who we are than with what we "accomplish."

Uzziah accomplished a great deal—enough for two or three lifetimes. I picture this guy out on the job from "can-see until can't-see," as Louis L'Amour used to put it. He was probably out with the troops, leading the attack on the stubborn Philistine bastions. He was there in his hard hat with a clipboard in his hand as he surveyed those huge construction projects. He was out walking in the fields and vineyards at first light, checking on the crops. He was crawling along the top of a newly built wall with a plumb line, while the nervous builders waited below. He was closeted with his generals late at night, poring over maps and scrolls and diagrams.

But in all this feverish busyness, he began to give his relationship with God lower and lower priority. He had been "marvelously helped" to become all he had become and do all he had done, but he began to forget just Who had helped him.

As a result, an emptiness began to fall across his life. The bustle and busyness, the full Daytimer and the tight deadlines were squeezing God right out of his heart and life.

There was a second reason for Uzziah's tragic fall that goes right along with the first: *Uzziah's character did not keep pace with his accomplishments.*

It's no different for us than it was for Uzziah; we all put a great amount of emphasis on the externals of life. We'll hear the phrase, "He's a successful businessman." What does that mean? Well, it means he's had an elevation in wealth, or in privilege, or in power. And you go by a newsstand and you see this man's mug on the cover of *Time* or *Fortune*. But—think about it—how many successful dads and husbands do we put on the cover of *Time?* Why don't we say, "Here's a guy who's got his priorities squared away. He's making a good living, but he's also making a good character. He doesn't have much of a financial portfolio, but he's spent a lot of time developing character in the lives of his kids. He's had a quiet, steady walk with God for thirty years."

One of the things about raising children is that you cannot impart that which you do not possess. I can't expect something out of my kids that does not exist in my own heart; character isn't something you mandate, it's something you model. And if you are spending your life chasing after external accomplishments rather than internal character, it will show. Count on it, friend, eventually *it will show.* Your kids may see the emptiness and superficial Christianity before you do, and by that time, it may be too late to show them a better way.

There is a third reason for Uzziah's disastrous mid-life collapse. His quick and rapid success became treacherous ice which caused him to lose equilibrium. In other words, *he was tripped up by his own success!*

Sometimes we get upset with the Lord because we are not as "successful" as we would like to be. We would like to be making a little more money or moving up the ladder at work a little bit faster. We'd like a little elevation in status to go along with our tenure on the job and our experience, but it seems terribly slow in coming.

Many times I believe this is nothing less than the grace of God. God is gracious when He does not answer our prayers for external success. (Remind me of this one, will you guys?) Because He knows very well how treacherous and dangerous that success can be. Success is like ice: it's beautiful, it's smooth, it looks clean and cool. But there aren't many men who can walk on ice without falling flat on their faces or flat on their duffs. Too many accomplishments and too much recognition too soon can be tragic. Not many of us can handle that kind of dangerous footing.

Uzziah, it turns out, couldn't handle it at all.

God knows when we can handle success and He knows when we can't. As a loving Father, He makes sure that He orders events in such a way that we can walk steadily along the road to heaven without slipping.

A friend of mine told me about taking his young children along a treacherous path in the mountains. They were walking along a steep embankment that plunged hundreds of feet to a frothy, churning stream below. Because it was early in the year, they ran into some ice along the path. He should have turned back right there, but he didn't. He wanted to show the kids a great waterfall at the end of the path. Like so many of us men, he was destination oriented. So they kept going, hanging on to a rusty cable at the side of that treacherous pathway.

God was gracious to my friend, and no one was hurt. But he winces now as he looks back on that hike. It was stupid to expose his young kids to that kind of danger. They could have easily slipped on the treacherous footing and plunged into the canyon below. They weren't old enough to handle it. He should have waited until they were older, or until a different season, or until they had the right equipment.

God is a good and wise Father, and He knows the trails well. When He keeps us off the dangerous trails of steep success and sudden wealth, we should thank Him and trust Him to do what's best for us. Sure, the prospects at the end of the success trail are exciting. But our Father doesn't want us to fall into a canyon on the way.

Warren Wiersbe has wisely said: "If God puts something in my hand without first doing something to my heart, my character will lag behind my achievements, and that is the way to ruin."

Scripture says of Uzziah...

> When he became strong, his heart was so proud that he acted corruptly. (v. 16)

If Uzziah hadn't been so busy building walls and canals, he might have remembered the stern words of one of his great-grandfathers, King Solomon:

Pride goes before destruction,

a haughty spirit before a fall. (Proverbs 16:18, NIV)

Pride is such a subtle thing. I usually don't recognize it in my life. In his classic book *Mere Christianity*, C. S. Lewis has a chapter called "The Greatest Sin in the World." With his characteristic insight and clarity, Lewis demonstrates that pride is that "greatest sin." He writes this incredible chapter that defines the right kind of pride ("I'm proud of my son") and the wrong kind of pride ("I have to be the best. I have to be number one.") And after discussing all the subtle nuances and ins and outs of pride, Lewis ends the chapter by stating: "If you have read this and you're convinced that this does not apply to you, then it certainly *does* apply to you." Whoa!

In other words, if you don't think that you struggle with pride, then you are the proudest person of all—and you are in great danger. See how subtle this is? Uzziah would have read that chapter by C. S. Lewis and thought to himself, "I sure am glad I don't struggle with that!" Even a man as great and strong and well taught as Uzziah fell victim to it. Who are you and I to say it couldn't trip us up, too?

At some point in his life, Uzziah gradually began to shift his trust from his God to his accomplishments. He began to shift his confidence in God to his confidence in military strength and innovations. He began to shift his delight in the Lord God of his fathers to a delight in his own accomplishments.

Uzziah could not handle his success; instead, his success handled him. It ruined him. Sometimes Satan waits forty years to spring a trap like this, but he's patient. If it takes waiting, he'll wait.

What did Uzziah actually do? Just listen:

His heart was so proud that he acted corruptly, and he was unfaithful to the LORD his God, for he entered the temple of the LORD to burn incense on the altar of incense. (v. 16)

In the insanity of his pride and presumption, Uzziah actually usurped the role of the priests and went charging into the temple to do that which he was never intended or allowed by Law to do. Talk about pride! How could he do such a presumptuous thing? The simple answer is that *pride blinds us*. C. S. Lewis had another great observation about pride when he said, "Pride is spiritual cancer; it eats the very possibility of love or contentment, or even common sense." Uzziah had cancer of the spiritual cornea. That's why he was blinded to the common sense he once possessed.

I remember reading the biography of the great English Bible teacher, Dr. Martyn Lloyd-Jones. Even though it has been a number of years since I cracked that book, one thing he said still burns in my memory. Every day of his life this man of God prayed the same prayer: "Lord, keep me from pride."

Since I read that, I've prayed the same way: *Lord, keep me from pride. Help me to recognize it. Help me to be aware of it. Help me not to be dazzled by it, seduced by it, intoxicated by it.*

I really believe this is one of those prayers that ought to be brought before the Lord every single day. I believe that we ought to have our accountability buddies get in our faces on this issue every time we meet. Why? Because this sin is so subtle and hard to detect. In a verse I cited earlier, the writer of the book of Hebrews says, "Encourage one another daily...so that none of you may be hardened by sin's deceitfulness" (Hebrews 3:13, NIV). Another way to say that might be, "Encourage one another daily, so that none of you may be *blinded* by sin's deceitfulness."

Pride is like a degenerative eye disease that gradually blinds you. But its progress is so slow you don't even realize you're losing your spiritual vision—until it's too late.

Imagine you could travel back in time, and you had the opportunity to take King Uzziah out for breakfast ten or fifteen years before his fall. You're sitting there over bagels and eggs, and you look into those bright, intelligent eyes across from you and say, "Hey, Uz. I have something to tell you, and you'll never believe it. But listen to this: within ten years, you will take a censer of sacred incense and go charging into the holy place of the temple to burn incense on the altar. In the process, you'll blow right by your chief priest and eighty other godly priests who will try to stop you."

Uzziah would laugh you out of the restaurant. That little scenario would seem utterly ridiculous to him. Unbelievable. Incomprehensible. Irrational. When he stopped laughing, he would say, "Listen, friend, you can relax. I could *never* do such a thing!"

Yet blinded by pride, that's exactly what he did. And he paid the price.

Uzziah knew the Scriptures. He knew that God's Law strictly forbade anyone to burn incense at that altar but one of the priests. He knew that he was violating the worship of God. It made no sense at all. It would be like robbing the local 7-11 store at gunpoint, taking three thousand dollars, and then going to church and dropping it in the offering. There's no way that's going to please God, and deep down Uzziah knew better.

But he had become blind. He couldn't even see the old familiar things he had known from childhood. He was blind and in great danger of slipping off the icy path and falling headlong into a canyon.

How do you know if you're going blind with pride? Well, you might watch for a few tell-tale symptoms.

SYMPTOMS OF PRIDE

ARROGANCE

First, note that somewhere in his meteoric rise to fame, he developed an attitude of arrogance. What is arrogance? The dictionary defines arrogance as being "haughty." That's an old French word which means "high." We get haughty when we think too highly of ourselves. We become arrogant when we convince ourselves we "deserve" certain perks and privileges.

Every now and then it's fun having a special privilege or two. The problem comes when you begin to *expect* the privilege—and find yourself getting upset when it's not there. Not long ago I heard of a senior missionary in the Philippines who became extremely angry when a more junior missionary inadvertently parked in the older man's parking space at their urban Manila mission head-quarters. To this day, the man who accidentally usurped his senior's "privilege" feels the pain when he remembers the loud, humiliating dressing-down he received that day. Over a lousy parking space!

But that's what arrogance does. You begin to expect certain privileges in your life and feel angry or bitter when they don't fall your way. If you don't get those mints on your pillow, if someone takes your parking space, if someone forgets to acknowledge your part, if you don't see your name when the credits roll, you get your nose out of joint. That's a first step toward the blindness of pride.

When you study the surrounding cultures of Uzziah's day, many of the other kings also had the privilege and prerogative of acting as priests. It may be that Uzziah looked around at some of the things his contemporaries were doing and thought, *Why can't I be a priest AND a king like these other guys? Are they better than I am?* Yet it was a direct violation of God's ways and God's commands. Uzziah knew it, but in his blindness he just couldn't see it anymore.

There is a second serious symptom that closely follows the first.

AVERSION TO ACCOUNTABILITY

Note what happens in verses seventeen and eighteen:

> Then Azariah the priest entered after him and with him eighty priests
> of the LORD, valiant men. And they opposed Uzziah the king and said
> to him, "It is not for you, Uzziah, to burn incense to the LORD, but for
> the priests, the sons of Aaron who are consecrated to burn incense. Get
> out of the sanctuary, for you have been unfaithful, and will have no
> honor from the LORD God."

How did Uzziah respond to these valiant priests of the Lord? His response is tragic.

> But Uzziah, with a censer in his hand for burning incense, was
> enraged. (v. 19)

There was no accountability in this man's life. And when some godly men tried to face off with him and stop him in his headlong plunge into disaster, he exploded in a rage.

Without question, when I look at spiritual leaders who have fallen into immorality, the one thing they all have in common is that somewhere in their lives they've brushed aside any accountability to brothers in Christ. Being accountable is a willingness to explain your actions. And do you know what? Every one of us needs the discipline of explaining our actions at various times in our lives. Every one of us needs a godly friend or two who are willing to confront us and say, "What are you doing? Why are you heading in that direction? Why are you acting that way? Why are you spending your time like that? Why are you messing around with that kind of stuff? There's danger ahead if you don't turn around!"

Do you have guys like that in your life—guys like the "valiant men" who confronted a powerful, pride-blinded king in the temple? How do you respond when they get in your way and ask you tough questions? If you find yourself getting very angry, if you find yourself wanting to pull away from accountability—beware! You're a long ways down the wrong road.

Every one of us needs friends who love us enough to make us explain our actions. That's a safeguard, a safety net for us. As my friend Stu Weber says, that kind of friend is like a guardrail on a narrow road through the mountains.

WHAT IF...?

For me, reading the Bible spawns a lot of "what if" questions. What if this had happened instead of that? What if Adam had refused a bite of the fruit Eve brought him? What if Noah had not been a man who walked with God? What if Pontius Pilate had released Jesus instead of handing him over to be crucified?

And what if—when he was confronted with the truth by his priests in the temple—Uzziah had come to his senses and dropped to his knees and said, "Oh God...forgive me! I repent of this foolishness and sin!"

Knowing God's character, I think I know what would have happened. God's grace is sufficient. I believe Uzziah would have walked out of the temple unmarked—and a better man.

But that's not what happened. Here's what did:

> But Uzziah, with a censer in his hand for burning incense, was
> enraged; and while he was enraged with the priests, the leprosy broke
> out on his forehead before the priests in the house of the LORD, beside
> the altar of incense.... King Uzziah was a leper to the day of his death;
> and he lived in a separate house, being a leper, for he was cut off from
> the house of the LORD. (vv. 19, 21)

There were at least four terrible consequences to Uzziah's prideful sin. There are always consequences, aren't there? God promises that there will be; He will not be mocked. We may not see them right away, and we might not understand all the implications of those consequences to the lives of our wives and children, but there will be consequences all the same.

THE FALLOUT FROM UZZIAH'S PRIDE

Number one, as we've seen, Uzziah was struck with the loathsome disease of leprosy for the rest of his life. That would put a dent in anyone's pride. Anyone who saw the man's face—eaten as it was by leprosy—would be overcome by revulsion and want to turn away.

Second, he lived in quarantine for the rest of his life. Uzziah had always enjoyed being a part of everything...but now he was cut off. Most likely, he had no servants. No one waiting on him. No special privileges. No mints on his pillow. No reserved parking space for his royal chariot. After enjoying a five-star lifestyle through all his adult life, he became like a lonely hermit, scrounging for himself.

Third, he was cut off from the temple. The great temple, lovingly constructed by Solomon and the spiritual resting place of the God of Israel for generations, was central to the life and worship of Judah. And Uzziah, who in his presumption and pride had treated the holiness of that temple with contempt, was now excluded for the rest of his life. He had thought to take himself into the holiest place; now, he would never even get past the threshold. And it never had to happen! But he let pride get a grip on his life. Moody was right: "God sends no one away empty except those who are full of themselves."

Finally, Uzziah was buried near the kings, but not with them.

> Uzziah rested with his fathers and was buried near them in a field for
> burial that belonged to the kings, for people said, "He had leprosy."
> (v. 23, NIV)

Even in death, his memory was dishonored. Now that doesn't seem quite fair, does it? After all he had accomplished for Judah...after all he had built...after all he had conquered...after all the years of wise and far-sighted administration...he would be remembered by small and great as "the king who had leprosy."

Fair or not, that's the way it generally works, isn't it? You and I both probably know men who labored faithfully for the Lord for many years before they fell away. They wrote best-selling books. They preached at great conferences. They were on hundreds of radio stations every day. Yet what are they remembered for? *"Oh, that's the guy who ran off with his secretary. That's the guy who left his church and family."*

I don't want to be remembered that way after I die. I don't want my kids to remember me that way. I don't want my wife to remember me that way. I don't want my friends to remember me that way. I want to finish strong...and I have a hunch that you do, too.

What can we learn from this biography of a successful man who started strong but fell out of the race?

External accomplishments can be false indicators of success.

We all probably know better…but all of us do it anyway. We judge by what we see. We evaluate by first impression. We form conclusions on the basis of outward appearances. God knows our tendency to make such judgments. That's why He warns us consistently against it. As He gently told Samuel when the old prophet was ready to anoint the wrong man as king:

> "Do not consider his appearance or his height, for I have rejected him. The LORD does not look at the things man looks at. Man looks at the outward appearance, but the LORD looks at the heart." (1 Samuel 16:7, NIV)

You and I tend toward the same thing, don't we? We look at some guy's build, or his tailored suit, or his luxury car, or his track record of accomplishments, and compare ourselves. We find ourselves wishing we could have what he has or do what he does or speak like he speaks or make money like he makes money. But that's what Uzziah's contemporaries would have said, too! "Man, if I could only be like Uzziah! If I could only have my act together half as well as he!"

But we never know what's happening on the *inside*, do we? We can't see into a man's character, the way God sees. So we call one man "successful" who is really not a success at all and is on a path to disaster and heartbreak. And we call another man an "also ran" or a "failure" because he doesn't seem to measure up in our eyes.

But God can already see the finish line. He knows already who will finish strong…and who won't.

We should beware of spiritual indifference.

Blindness to spiritual things doesn't come first. Arrogance and presumption don't come first. There is something that comes before these things; there is something that provides the necessary soil for these poisonous plants to germinate and grow. And that something is spiritual indifference. It's an ever-so-gradual cooling of your spiritual temperature. It's an ever-so-subtle fading of your love for the Lord Jesus. It's as silent and subtle as a slow moving shadow. One minute you're sitting in the sun, reading your newspaper, and enjoying the warmth and radiance. Then suddenly you feel cool, and you look up and realize you've been sitting in the shade for some time. The sun and warmth have long since passed by.

You're not seeking Jesus Christ the way you once did.

You're not hungrily diving into the Word the way you once did.

You're not enjoying the company of other believers the way you once did.

You're not delighting in quiet walks and talks with God the way you once did.

You're in the shadow, a long way from the Son, and you don't even know how you got there or how your heart became so cold.

It's not too late to move back into the sunlight! It's not too late to turn away from false standards of "success" and seek the Lord with all your heart. How did Paul put it?

> Never be lacking in zeal, but keep your spiritual fervor, serving the
> Lord. (Romans 12:11, NIV)

Uzziah started so well, lived up to so much of his potential, but finished out of the race. Why? Because he got suckered by pride. The greatest sin. As Lewis put it:

> The essential vice, the utmost evil, is pride. Unchastity, anger, greed,
> drunkenness, and all that, are mere fleabites in comparison. It was
> through pride that the devil became the devil. Pride leads to every
> other vice; it is the complete anti-God state of mind.

Ask God to open your eyes and show you your pride. And be prepared that He may use your wife, or your kids, or a friend to point it out to you. And ask Him to give you the grace not to be defensive when they tell you.

Ask God to give you the courage to face it.

And deal with it.

And crush it.

Every day.

CHAPTER SIX

UNTEACHABLE, UNACCOUNTABLE, AND UNACCEPTABLE

———————○

When a man is wrapped up in himself,
he makes a pretty small package.

JOHN RUSKIN

The only reason I picked the guy in the first place was because I'd never heard of him.

I was twenty-two years old, in my first year of seminary. One of my professors had just given us an unusual assignment. We were supposed to come up with a sermon on someone in the Bible we'd never heard of.

I figured a good place to start was in a book of the Bible I'd hardly ever read.

Sure enough, down in verse nine of the little book of 3 John, I stumbled across the name of Diotrephes.

Perfect. I'd never heard a lick about this guy.

I spent several weeks studying the life of this man who rates two verses in Scripture...and I think it was about the best thing that could have happened to me at that tender age. I remember coming away from that experience just shaking my head. *Lord,* I found myself praying, *I never, never want to be like that man. God help me never to end up like that.*

I was single at the time—no wife, no family, no job, no ministry. It was the time of life when a young man could really benefit from some positive role models. But the truth is, I think I benefited more that year from one negative role model than a half-dozen positive ones. Diotrephes is a classic prototype for a young, would-be leader. All you have to do is carefully study the stuff he did...and then go out and do the exact opposite.

Years ago, Seven-Up introduced a memorable ad campaign. It was success-ful for so long that they recently resurrected it. They proudly called themselves "the UnCola," and it gave them immediate positioning in the marketplace. The ads really didn't do that much to describe the company's product; instead, they made it clear what their soda was NOT. Hey, we're *not* a cola. We're *not* root beer. We're the UnCola. The sales of Seven-Up enjoyed a huge surge...because of the way they chose to NOT describe their beverage.

The critical word was "un."

Now what does the word "un" mean in the Greek? Frankly, I don't know. You'll just have to trust me here. When I look at that prefix "un," it seems to suggest two things: different and opposite.

That year I learned quite a bit about leadership. The professors worked hard to show us what true biblical leadership was all about. But one UnLeader with a funny name showed me even more. And I have a tiny little letter from an old man named John to thank for that.

A LETTER FROM DEAR JOHN

Third John, of course, is the third letter from the man known as "the Beloved Apostle." As you might imagine, getting a letter from an apostle—one of the Twelve—was a big deal back in the first century. It must have been especially impressive to receive something from John. Good old John. This was the guy who was closer to the Lord Jesus than anyone else, a man who always seemed to be at the Lord's side.

When a letter like this arrived, the church would assemble and one of the elders would read it out loud. In this particular letter—really, it was more like a quick postcard—there were some words that must have had folks nudging each other and exchanging meaningful glances. I have the idea that John's little epistle went off like an M-80 in that assembly of believers. And when the smoke cleared, everyone realized that the elderly apostle had no intention of tiptoeing around what must have been a highly sensitive issue in that congregation. He had some strong words about a man in their midst who wanted very badly to be a leader...but was, in fact, an UnLeader. Just as Seven-Up is the UnCola, so Diotrephes was the UnLeader.

Quite frankly, he was a jerk.

> I wrote to the church, but Diotrephes, who loves to be first, will have nothing to do with us. So if I come, I will call attention to what he is doing, gossiping maliciously about us. Not satisfied with that, he refuses to welcome the brothers. He also stops those who want to do so and puts them out of the church. (vv. 9–10, NIV)

One of the best definitions of a leader I ever heard was also one of the shortest. Dr. Howard Hendricks offered this one, and it's only six words long. I can get a handle on a definition like that! And here it is. Ready? *A leader is someone who leads.* That definition is so good that I have quoted it probably five hundred times. And I'll probably quote it another five hundred.

That's it. That's all of it. A leader is someone who leads. But don't let the simplicity fool you. Really, it's profound. Just because you have a *title* of leadership doesn't mean that you are a leader. You're only a leader if you lead. A number of months ago at a business luncheon in Dallas, a distinguished looking gentleman handed me his card. It may have been the most impressive business card I've ever seen. It was embossed in gold on silky white stock, and the thing was half-filled up with this guy's titles. You can't believe all the stuff this man had under his name. He was CEO, CFO, President, Chairman, Emperor, Ayatollah, His Excellency...it went on and on.

As time went by, I became more familiar with this man and what he did. I talked to people who worked for him. I picked up things about his reputation in the community. And do you know what I found out? He wasn't a leader at all. Sure, he had a title—he had a list of 'em long as your arm. But titles of leadership don't make you a leader. You're only a leader if you lead, and no one was willing to call this man a leader. No one was marching in his one-man parade.

You might have the title…President…but do you lead?

You might have the title…Quarterback…but do you lead?

You might have the title…Team Captain…Platoon Leader…Principal…Teacher…Pastor…Elder…Husband…Dad. That's great. Those are all honorable titles. But listen—you're only a leader if you *lead*. Diotrephes was a man who wanted to be a leader—he wanted it so bad he could taste it. When he looked in the bathroom mirror in the morning, he thought for sure he was looking at a leader. But he wasn't a leader at all. We don't know what his official position might have been in the church—obviously, he had some clout or power. But a leader? A Christian leader? Not on your life. Diotrephes was the UnLeader. Let me explain why.

FIVE MARKS OF THE UNLEADER

Lots of people have written about the marks of a leader. I have pages of notes in my files that I could dig out of my basement if you'd like to see more. But this is kind of an UnChapter, and I'd rather look at this leadership thing from the other side; I want to show you the clear marks of an UnLeader. What makes an UnLeader?

Notice what John says in verse nine:

> I wrote something to the church; but Diotrephes, who loves to be first
> among them…

You've got to remember something about John. He was one of those guys who went to Bible school and never got over it. If you were to sit down with

John over a glass of iced tea, he'd bend your ear until next Tuesday talking about his great education as a young man. If anyone else went on and on like that, it would be about as exciting as watching ice melt on warm linoleum.

But then, I guess you might excuse ol' John for his enthusiasm. He really *did* have a great education. The best. Because his only professor for those years was the Lord Jesus Christ.

John was staggered by Jesus. That's the way it is with people who hang out with the Lord day after day. They can't stop talking about Him. They can't help looking at every issue the way He would look at that issue. And when a guy's spent forty-two straight months walking alongside the King of kings and Lord of lords, he's bound to have a few impressions on certain subjects. Think about it. Think about eating meals over the campfire with Him...rowing a boat with Him into the teeth of a storm...confronting dangerous enemies with Him... praying with Him on a mountainside...meeting men's and women's deep needs with Him...sleeping under the stars with Him...walking on the beach with Him at sunrise...watching Him lose His life on a cross...staring at Him until your eyes blur as He ascends into the blue heavens.

To tell the truth, John never got over those forty-two months with Jesus. Even when he wrote his gospel, he had a tough time ending it. How do you end a book about someone who has no end? How do you put a period on an infinite story? John finally saw that he had to wrap things up, and it's a good thing; otherwise you and I would be packing our Bibles around in a wheelbarrow. I'm guessing he scratched out these last words with a deep sigh:

> Jesus did many other things as well. If every one of them were written
> down, I suppose that even the whole world would not have room for
> the books that would be written. (John 21:25, NIV)

So here's a man brimming over with the teachings of Jesus, and he has to confront a would-be leader who isn't acting like Jesus at all. Which leads us to the first mark of an UnLeader.

Mark #1: An UnLeader is an UnServant.

What did Jesus say about leadership?

> "If any one wants to be first, he shall be last of all, and servant of all."
> (Mark 9:35)
>
> "Whoever then humbles himself as this child, he is the greatest in
> the kingdom of heaven." (Matthew 18:4)
>
> "Whoever wishes to become great among you shall be your
> servant, and whoever wishes to be first among you shall be your slave;
> just as the Son of Man did not come to be served, but to serve, and to
> give His life a ransom for many." (Matthew 20:26–28)

John had no problem at all nailing Diotrephes as an UnLeader. Do you know why? Because Diotrephes wasn't leading like Jesus. And for John, that pretty much fried the man's bacon.

One thing that sets apart Christian leadership from any other type of leadership is the idea of being a *servant*. Someone once asked Leonard Bernstein, the late New York Symphony conductor, what the most difficult position in the orchestra was. Without hesitation, the maestro replied, "Second fiddle." Now why is that? Is playing second-chair violin so much tougher than playing a piccolo or a bassoon? No, it's not tougher. His point was, everyone wants to be *first-chair* violin.

Ask a budding young musician his or her goal in life. What's the reply going to be? "Oh, I really want to be second chair violin someday." Probably not.

Do you know any young boys who want to grow up to become a second string quarterback? Not likely.

You see, nobody wants to be second. Everyone wants to be first. Diotrephes was strongly motivated to be number one. But the problem is, that runs completely against the grain of Christian leadership. *Christian leadership is giving your best without having to be first.*

As I studied Diotrephes, I got concerned. Real concerned. About me. The more I studied Diotrephes, the more I saw I was a lot like him. It was uncanny.

Diotrephes loved to be first. I didn't want to admit it, but so did I.

Diotrephes liked being served. I didn't want to admit it, but so did I.

Diotrephes enjoyed being a big shot.

Diotrephes got a kick out of special privileges.

Diotrephes liked to impress people.

I didn't want to admit it, but so did I.

So it began to dawn on me that if I wanted to lead like Jesus instead of like Diotrephes, I was going to have to make some changes in my life. We're talking *drastic* changes. That's one of the biggest problems with reading the Bible. Every time I crack it open, I keep getting the idea that God wants me to change. I keep getting the idea that He wants to conform me into the image of Christ. God wants me to lead like Jesus, but I'm a whole lot more like the UnLeader.

A lot of us don't like change. It kind of bugs us. It isn't comfortable. That may date back to the time when we were little boys and didn't like to change our socks or underwear. But you see, if we're going to grow up in Christ, we've got to change every day. If we don't, we're not growing up in Christ...we're just growing old in Christ. And who wants to do that?

You know how many psychologists it takes to change a light bulb? Just one, but the light bulb must *want* to change. That's not really true, is it? Light bulbs obviously don't have to want to change, but people do. Men do.

Let me ask you a question: Do you want to change? Are you willing to change? Are you willing to become a servant? Unless I miss my guess, that serving stuff may not come naturally for you. It may not be your knee-jerk reaction to situations in your life. It's certainly not in mine. But do you know what? I really don't have an option. I'm *called* to do it.

Now, do you believe that God has a sense of humor? I can guarantee that He does. In fact, let me prove it to you. Do you see the last sentence of the previous paragraph? The sentence says, "I'm called to do it." Just as I was finishing this last sentence of the previous paragraph, I heard the faint words, "Daaaad... Daaaaad...." I walked out of my office to see my son vomiting in the hallway between his bedroom and the bathroom. And since I am here alone with my son, the job of serving him fell to me. In the last ninety minutes—when I should have been completing this chapter—I have cleaned up my son, put him to bed, cleaned up the vomit off the carpet, gone to the grocery store, rented a carpet shampooer, shampooed the carpet…well, you get the idea.

It is now 9:48 P.M. This completed chapter needs to be at FedEx by 10:30 P.M. So, FedEx closes in forty-two minutes.

When my son threw up, my first question was, "Where is Mary?" Actually that's not quite right. My first question was "WHERE IS MARY? *She promised on our wedding day to be faithful in sickness and in health—and THIS IS SICKNESS!*" Now, I didn't say this out loud. But I was thinking it.

After I cleaned Josh up and got him to bed, I looked at my watch and noticed that the time was quickly coming when "no man shall work."

I began to think, *Where is that woman and what is she doing? I don't have time to clean this crud up! I have to get this chapter done and get it to FedEx! I have to finish this section on servanthood so that these guys can be the men Christ wants them to be! Where is she? I'm about ready to throw up myself after getting this stuff off the carpet! I'm supposed to be doing something important for the kingdom of God instead of getting recycled hot dogs and chili off this rug!*

When I finally sat down to figure out where I left off, I noticed the last paragraph that I had written:

> Let me ask you a question: Do you want to change? Are you willing to change? Are you willing to become a servant? Unless I miss my guess, that serving stuff may not come naturally for you. It may not be your knee-jerk reaction to situations in your life. It's certainly not in mine. But do you know what? I really don't have an option. I'm *called* to do it.

Bingo. You see guys, it's easy for me to write this stuff. I just have a hard time living it. I'm more like Diotrephes than I like to admit.

Diotrephes resented being a servant, and that's how he got his first mark as an UnLeader. So far, I'm keeping up with him. But don't hang up the phone yet. There's another mark of an UnLeader.

Mark #2: An UnLeader is UnTeachable.

Catch this little note from John's postcard:

> I wrote something to the church; but Diotrephes, who loves to be first
> among them, *does not accept what we say.* (v. 9)

The guy was UnTeachable. Who was writing this letter, after all? It wasn't Joe Schmuck from the branch office. This was the *Apostle* John. A man handpicked by the Son of God. A man with impeccable authority. But Diotrephes didn't have any time for him. He wouldn't respond to John's leadership or teaching.

When I was a kid, I can remember telling anyone who would listen, "I can't wait until I grow up and *nobody* will tell me what to do."

But guess what? I'm forty-five years old and now *everyone's* telling me what to do. The IRS tells me what to do. The state of Texas tells me what to do. The department of motor vehicles tells me what to do. I've got all kinds of people in my life now that I'm "grown up," and most of them are telling me what to do. That's kind of the way life works for most of us.

What we're talking about here is a teachable spirit. Great leaders have teachable spirits. Great leaders know how to submit to authority. See, a lot of people have leadership inclinations. But they don't want to submit to anybody. They want to do it their way.

A couple of years ago, I was driving fifty-eight miles-per-hour in a thirty-mile zone. A guy pulled up behind me in a white car. The problem was, he had two options on his car that I didn't have on mine. And he turned them both on. I looked in the rearview mirror and thought to myself, *I need to do a little submitting to authority here. I need to work on having a teachable spirit.*

So I pulled over and this man in a uniform came up to my window and said, "Sir, can I ask where it is that you're in such a hurry to get to?"

One of my boys piped up from the backseat, "We're going to church!"

It was a Wednesday night and I was supposed to be teaching at one of the churches in Dallas. But the car was very low on fuel. It was a diesel, and it's not always easy to find diesel—anyway, it's a long story. The bottom line was that it was five minutes till seven, and I was thirty minutes away from the place where I was supposed to preach at seven o'clock.

"Oh," said the officer. "You're going to church?" He glanced down at the Bible I had beside me in the front seat.

"Yeah," I said, "I'm going across town to teach on Romans 13 about obeying the civil authorities."

The policeman started laughing. I think he must have been a believer, because he knew what was in Romans 13.

"I'll tell you what," he said. "If you promise to obey Romans 13, I'll let you go."

And I said, "That is mercy. Not justice, but mercy."

So I had to practice what I was going to preach before I ever preached it— even though it was going to make me late. But that's all a part of being teachable and submitting to authority. Diotrephes didn't give a rip for John, the elders, or apostolic authority. No one was going to tell *him* anything. He just flat wouldn't hear it. He wasn't teachable.

Mary and I speak together maybe once or twice a year. That's about all we can do because we don't like to dump off our kids with someone else. Several years ago we were speaking to a group of about eight hundred college students at a conference in Colorado. Eight hundred bright, fresh-faced guys and gals looked up at us from the auditorium, and we had a fun time talking about how to have a great marriage. That's not one of the usual topics when you're talking to collegians—but it ought to be. Because down the road, most of them will be getting married and won't have a clue how good marriages work.

Between sessions, four young women—seniors at the University of Nebraska—came up to talk to me.

"This won't take a lot of your time," they told me. "We just have one quick question."

"Sure," I said. "Fire away."

"We hope to be married one day," they told me. "Could you tell us—what one trait should we look for in a potential husband?"

I was tempted to tease them and say, "Money!" but they looked serious about this, so I thought I'd better not mess around. After thinking about it for a few seconds, I said, "The one trait you ought to look for in a potential husband is...*teachability*. Because if you find a guy who has a teachable spirit, he's going to be OK. All of us guys have our rough edges, and some of us are rougher than others. But a teachable guy will listen to your input. He'll be a big enough man to admit he's got lots of room for improvement. More importantly, he will be open to input from the Holy Spirit. He'll know how to humble himself before the Lord. A teachable guy is a guy who will grow up in Christ. If you find a guy like that, ladies, snap him up."

"Oh," said one. "Well, I'm not sure there are any guys out there like that."

"Yes, they're out there. The thing is, you only need one. If you needed ten or twenty, you might have a problem, but you only need one."

Let's put it on the table. If you're not teachable, you don't have a chance in the world of finishing strong. Not a chance.

A man in a small Wisconsin city had been in A.A. for about three years and had enjoyed being sober for that period of time. Then bad luck began to hit him in his business. The firm for which he had worked for some fifteen years was sold; his particular job was phased out of existence; and the plant was moved to another city. For several months, he struggled at odd jobs while looking for a company that needed his specialized experience.

Then another blow hit him. His wife was forced to enter a hospital for major surgery, and his company insurance expired. At this point he cracked and decided on an all-out binge. He didn't want to stage this in the small city where everyone knew his sobriety record. So he went to Chicago, checked into a north side hotel, and set forth on his project. It was Friday night, and the bars were filled with swinging crowds. But he was in no mood to swing—he just wanted to get quietly, miserably drunk.

Finally, he found a basement bar on a quiet side street, practically deserted. He sat down on a bar stool and ordered a double bourbon on the rocks. The bartender said, "Yes, sir," and reached for a bottle.

Then the bartender stopped in his tracks, took a long, hard look at the customer, leaned over the bar, and said in a low tone, "I was in Milwaukee about four months ago, and one night I attended an open A.A. meeting. You were on the speaking platform, and you gave one of the finest talks I ever heard." The bartender turned and walked to the end of the bar.

For a few minutes, the guy sat there—probably in a state of shock. With trembling hands, he picked up his money from the bar and walked out. All desire for a drink had been drained out of him.

It is estimated that there are about eight thousand saloons in Chicago, employing some twenty-five thousand bartenders. This man had entered the one saloon in eight thousand where he would encounter the one man in twenty-five thousand who knew that he was a member of A.A. and didn't belong there.

As far as I know, the man who had this amazing experience did not know the Lord. But I will tell you this. The Lord was looking out for him. He heard the message quite clearly. And he did something about it. Why? Because he was teachable.[1]

Mark #3: An UnLeader is UnJust.

It would have been enough for Diotrephes to be an UnServant and UnTeachable. But he was also UnJust. Look at verse ten:

> For this reason, if I come, I will call attention to his deeds which he
> does, unjustly accusing us with wicked words.

That's pretty serious stuff. Diotrephes was getting into deep trouble with his tongue. Isn't it amazing? Here's John, an apostle of Jesus Christ, one of the original Twelve, with the authority of Jesus Christ behind him, and Diotrephes has the gall to start throwing out off-the-wall accusations against him. Do you know what that tells me? If he was willing to level that kind of stuff at an apostle, this was not the first time he had pulled this sort of thing. There must have been many men and women who'd been wounded by the torpedoes launched out of this man's mouth. It was a habit of life for Diotrephes. It came as natural to him as kicking the dog. Actually, some people are a lot more humane to their dogs than they are to humans.

Diotrephes knew how to hurl verbal bombs. Maybe he did it with the acid of sarcasm. Maybe he did it with the poison of innuendoes and gossip. Or maybe he just stood up in front of the people and told bald-faced lies. However he did it, it was sin, and John called him on it. It's "wicked" the apostle said. And so it is.

More than anything else, spoken words determine the atmosphere of a home. Every home has an atmosphere. Just like restaurants have atmospheres. When most of us guys go into a restaurant, we could care less about the atmosphere. We just want a decent plate of food and refills on the drinks. But my wife sees it a little differently. When we go out on a special occasion, she wants something more than good food; she wants to go to a restaurant with *ambiance*. Do you know what ambiance means in French? I have decided it means *expensive*. The greater the ambiance, the greater the check. That's just how it works.

So good restaurants have a good atmosphere. But so do good homes. Generally speaking, your home either has an atmosphere of *construction* or *destruction*. In other words, people in your home are either being built up or they're being torn down. What kind of home were you raised in? Was it an atmosphere of construction or destruction?

It was Ring Lardner who said, "The family you come from is not as important as the family you are going to have." He's right. The truth is, I can't do anything about the home which I was born into. In my case, it was a good one. But now that I'm the dad, it's on *my* shoulders to make a good home.

What's going to be the atmosphere of my home? More than anything else, it will be my words that spell the difference between construction and destruction. What kind of words will echo off the walls of my home and sink into the souls of those impressionable folks under my roof? Unjust words like, "You'll never amount to anything." Unjust statements like, "Here, give me that wrench! You look so darned awkward with that thing."

I talked to a guy just this week whom I consider to be a highly gifted individual. I've known him for a long time and have worked closely with him. You know what he said to me? He said, "I feel kind of awkward about a lot of things—and I think I'm awkward because my dad always *told* me I was awkward."

I said, "You're not awkward at all." But he thinks that he is, because someone unjustly accused him. Somebody said some harsh words to him. Words are awesomely powerful instruments—for evil or good. And in a Christian home, there is no room for unjust words. We need to think about the words before they come spilling out of our faces. We need to ask ourselves, "Am I being just here? Is that a constructive remark? Or am I just trying to score a point?" As men who want to finish strong, we need to make sure our remarks and comments are constructive—and just.

Diotrephes had a problem with unjust accusations. But there is yet another "un" to consider in this brief little passage. And it may surprise you.

Mark #4: An UnLeader is UnHospitable.

UnHospitable? Inhospitable? What does that have to do with anything? What's the big deal about hospitality? Actually, it's amazing what a big deal hospitality is in the Scriptures. Hospitality goes hand in hand with a servant spirit. Look at the middle part of verse ten. John wrote:

> And not satisfied with this, neither does he himself receive the
> brethren, and he forbids those who desire to do so, and puts them out
> of the church.

You know, back in those days you couldn't put up a visiting teacher in the local Howard Johnson's. They didn't have hotels and motels and inns like we have today. Oh, they had overnight accommodations, all right. But most of *those* inns had red lights hanging over the front door, and that's not the place you want to send your visiting evangelists. So as John, an elder and apostle of the early church, would send out teachers to different locations, it was vital for the believers to provide them lodging. It was not only nice, it was necessary!

How long would these visiting Bible teachers stay in an area? I'm not sure, but it very well could have been a long-term sort of deal. My hunch is that it wasn't always convenient for those folks who opened up their homes. That's the thing about hospitality. It *isn't* always convenient. It isn't always comfortable and handy. It doesn't always fit right in with our plans and our schedules.

Diotrephes was not hospitable. He didn't like making other people feel like number one at his house, because *he* wanted to be number one.

When Mary and I were first married, we lived in a tiny apartment in Los Angeles. After three or four months, her mom and dad visited us en route from Atlanta to Japan on a missions trip. We picked them up at the airport, had a nice little dinner at home, and then talked awhile until it was time to hit the sack.

That's when Mary said to them, "Steve and I want you to have our bed."

What? When did I say that?

That's what I felt like saying. What I actually said was, "Yeah, we want you to have our bed."

The truth is, I didn't want them to have our bed at all. I value my comfort. I value a good night's sleep. I want my bed, my bear, and my jammies. And then let me alone. What really bothered me more than giving up my bed was the knowledge of what that would mean: it would mean that Mary and I were going to have to sleep on that broken-down hide-a-bed in the living room.

It ticked me off, but what could I say? I smiled at my new in-laws and said, "Oh, right! Take our bed. We insist. We'll be fine. This is wonderful."

We got things all set up for them, said good night, and they shut the door.

Then I turned and looked at Mary.

"All right Mary," I hissed through clenched teeth, "what's the deal? You didn't talk to me about that. We never agreed to that. I don't want to spend the night on this crummy, lumpy hide-a-bed." And I just really railed on her. I couldn't believe she would do such a thing, and I demonstrated my maturity to my new bride by saying so right up front. This was, of course, a whole new side of me that she had never seen.

As time went on, however, I came to understand how Mary would have automatically given up her bed like that. Come to find out, she'd seen that kind of hospitality modeled through all of her growing up years. Hospitality was a daily experience in her family; it was just the expected thing.

Mary's dad is in the ministry, and though the family never had many extras, they were always willing to share with others. About twenty-five years ago, her folks built a two-story home in Georgia. They had just enough money to finish out the top floor but had to leave the ground floor unfinished. Little by little, her dad worked away at it over the months and years, until they finally had a nice, three-bedroom apartment downstairs. Why did they do that? To have more elbowroom? To increase the value of the home?

No. They did that so they could let needy families live there rent-free in emergency situations. Every time we went to visit them in Georgia there would be a different family sharing the home with them.

And this is the atmosphere Mary grew up in. No wonder she offered our bed. She probably thought it was the least she could do. This was a family willing to be inconvenienced, and that's a sign of spiritual maturity.

I think there is one more "un" in the life of this man Diotrephes. It's not in the text, but it could be there—and it makes sense that it would be there. I think all those "uns" add up to another very sad "un."

Mark #5: An UnLeader has an UnHappy family.

Pity Mrs. Diotrephes.

Pity little Diotrephes Junior.

Pity Diotrephes' in-laws, who probably had to lump it on the hide-a-bed.

Scripture doesn't tell us if he was married or not. Let's just assume for a minute that he was. You've got to believe that a person with those sorts of UnServantlike character qualities is going to have a miserably UnHappy family.

I want you to think this through with me. It was pretty severe for John to have to put those strong words in a letter that's read to the whole church. Do you think Diotrephes would have been out of the room for a public reading like this? Not him! He would have been right there on the front pew. And when John started rebuking Diotrephes, everyone would have looked straight at him. That's tough stuff, don't you think? Gentle and gracious John had taken the gloves off, and now he was sounding more like the old "son of thunder."

But I think those kinds of measures must have been necessary. Unless I miss my guess, I'll bet the Lord had tried to get through to this man in gentler ways. He had probably been trying to get Diotrephes' attention for years before this happened.

Imagine with me that Diotrephes had a wife. Do you think she might have tried to reason with him through the years? Do you think she might have tried to gently broach the subject of this man's stubborn attitude and harsh words? If Diotrephes had kids, do you think some tears were ever shed in this man's presence? Do you think those kids might have tried to talk to their dad about some of the unjust things he was saying? Do you think they did?

I believe that God also speaks to us today. I really do. I hear some preachers on TV always talking about this vision and that vision. But it seems like the only time I have a vision is if I eat Mexican food after 10 P.M. And God is not in that vision.

Does God speak to us today? You bet He does. He speaks to us in His Word. But He also has another way of getting through to us.

It's amazing how God will talk to me through my wife and my kids. And when I start hearing the same thing being said over and over again, I'd better listen up. If I want a happy family, I'd better listen to some of those words—and even some of those silences!

That's not easy for me. Just like you, I get into a groove. I get goal oriented and locked on course. At such times, it's not easy for me to pick up on my family's emotional needs. In the heat of the moment, it's easy for me to get upset and irritated and start throwing around harsh words. That is my natural tendency.

But deep down, I don't want to be an UnLeader. I don't want to be a Diotrephes who wouldn't listen to anyone—even God! I want to finish strong. I want to be like Jesus.

As you probably know, most of the names in the Bible have a meaning. Do you know what Diotrephes' name means in the original language? It means "nourished by Zeus." And Zeus was a false god.

We can have false gods in our lives, too. We can be nourished by gods other than the true and living God.

For some of us, it's the god of power.

For some of us, it's the god of popularity or fame.

For some of us, it's the drive to be number one.

If you and I want to finish strong, we need to be "nourished by Jesus Christ." We need to hear what He has to say to us, even if the words humble us and bruise our egos and take us down a couple of notches.

The bottom line is this: being an UnLeader is UnManly.

Real men *serve*. Just like Jesus did.

I'm working on it. If I'm going to finish strong, I *have* to work on it. And so do you. As we ask Christ to make us the teachable, accountable men that He wants us to be, we will begin to change.

Diotrephes was a jerk and didn't want to make the change.

But we still have time to change.

That's the UnChanged and UnBlemished truth.

PART THREE

THE PROTOTYPES OF FINISHING STRONG

CHAPTER SEVEN

LOUSY START, STRONG FINISH

If three people say you are an ass,
put on a bridle.

SPANISH PROVERB

This has been a tough book for some of you to read. And the reason it's been tough is because some of you, deep down inside your hearts, think that you have already disqualified yourselves from finishing strong.

Maybe you've committed adultery and left your wife for some other woman.

Maybe you've neglected your kids to the point that they don't even want to talk to you.

Maybe you're reading this in a prison cell—and you're honest enough to admit that you deserve to be there.

Or maybe you came to Christ later in life and simply feel that you've wasted too many years and lost too much ground. In other words, you think that you've already messed up your life so badly that you have no shot at ever finishing strong.

If that's what you're thinking, then hang in there with me through this next chapter. What you read may cause you to think again.

I learned a lot of good stuff in Sunday school. Maybe you did, too.

I learned about Daniel in the lions' den. I learned about those three Hebrew kids who got tossed into the furnace. I learned about Zacchaeus up in the tree, about Jonah and the big fish, and about the little boy who brought his lunch to Jesus. Come to think of it, I probably learned more in Sunday school than I learned in seminary. But in all that good teaching, there's one guy I never learned about.

They never told me about Manasseh.

But they *should* have. This guy Manasseh may have the most incredible story in the entire Bible. So why didn't they tell me about him?

Manasseh was a man Sunday school teachers seem to avoid. Frankly, he's not the kind of guy you want kids to know about. That's probably why his name never came up. In Sunday school they told me about Abraham, Isaac, Jacob, Joseph, Moses, and David. But Manasseh really doesn't fit in with those guys.

Manasseh fits in with guys like Attila the Hun, Adolf Hitler, Joseph Stalin, Idi Amin, and Saddam Hussein. I mean this guy was bad news. Real bad news. If you crossed Manasseh, you paid. And you paid big-time. Manasseh's favorite color was red—as in blood red. This guy had no mercy. He was hell on wheels. He had a hair-trigger for anyone who was interested in obeying God—because that was the one thing that he hated. This guy came out of a godly home with an ungodly hatred for God. In Manasseh, we see a man who ran what may have been the wickedest, bloodiest, and most rebellious race a man could ever run. But much later in life, Manasseh changed direction—by 180 degrees.

And amazingly, he finished strong.

I remember a big dude who came up to me a number of years ago. This guy had lived a hard life. Drugs, jail, more drugs, assault, more jail. And it all showed in his face. This guy didn't know the first thing about Christianity. All he knew about Jesus was that the Doobie Brothers thought Jesus was "just all right."

I had just finished speaking on the unbelievable grace and forgiveness of God. This guy came up to me and whispered in my ear, "What if you've broken *all* of the Ten Commandments?" In other words, this man wanted to know if the grace of God and the forgiveness of God could cover *everything*.

It does. It really does. If it doesn't, we're all out of business. I don't care who you are, or what you have done, or how evil you have been. If God could forgive Manasseh, He can forgive you. I'll show you just what I mean.

THE LIFESTYLE OF MANASSEH

We all make choices every day about the way we live our lives. If you're reading these words and you're alive, you're making choices. And some of the most significant, life-shaping choices you will ever make will come in the course of what seems like ordinary, everyday living. That's why it pays to walk with God moment by moment.

But Manasseh did not walk with God. He started off on his own path very early in life, and kept at it until it was very late.

But not too late.

Scripture begins the account of his life like this:

> Manasseh was twelve years old when he became king. (2 Kings 21:1)

That's a young age to become a king. I've tried to picture my son Joshua as a king at the age of twelve, but somehow, I just can't see it. I picture skateboards and baseball cards and Nintendo games...not a young man sitting on a throne with total power in his hands. Manasseh actually co-ruled with his father, Hezekiah, in those early years. It was sort of an apprentice deal. But when Hezekiah died, Manasseh had the whole kingdom. Verse one goes on to tell us:

> He reigned fifty-five years in Jerusalem.

That's a long time in office by anyone's standards. But they didn't have "term limits" in Judah in those days, so they were basically stuck with this guy. He had an unbelievable influence for over half a century in the nation. If you really work at it, you can do a fair amount of damage in fifty-five years. For that matter, you can do significant harm in just four years. Imagine having a corrupt, immoral, God-hating, Christian-hating president over the United States of America. Now imagine him being in office from 1945 until the year 2000. A guy could make his mark on the country in that length of time. And Manasseh certainly made his. The next verse gets more specific about his lifestyle:

> And he did evil in the sight of the LORD, according to the abominations
> of the nations whom the LORD dispossessed before the sons of Israel.
> (v. 2)

Now what is this talking about? Well, number one, it says he did evil. And he did the kind of evil that was in the Promised Land—the land of Canaan—before Joshua and his troops arrived on the scene to wipe out the Canaanites at God's specific command. Sexual perversion and child sacrifice were everyday stuff among these people.

But judgment day fell for the Canaanites, just as it will fall for all the nations of the world. And God is telling us in 2 Kings that what Manasseh did in Judah was the same kind of sick stuff the Canaanites were addicted to before they were driven out of the land. The phrase in the text "according to the abominations of the nations" simply means that as perverse and violent as the Canaanites were, they had nothing on Manasseh. He *equaled* their perversion.

Verse three gives us some more background:

> For he rebuilt the high places which Hezekiah his father had destroyed.

The high places were just that. They were places on the tops of hills, little groves that had been carved out for "religious" ceremonies. But let me clue you: they weren't having church picnics or softball games up there. They weren't worshiping the God of Israel. While Manasseh was rebuilding the high places, he also

> ...erected altars for Baal and made an Asherah, as Ahab king of Israel
> had done, and worshiped all the host of heaven and served them. (v. 3)

Manasseh wouldn't allow the worship of the Lord. He probably fought hard to keep the Ten Commandments from being posted in public schools. Manasseh believed in religious diversity, and he was more than happy to accommodate the worship of any number of pagan religions. Baal was one of the king's favorites Asherah was right up there, too. An Asherah was a wooden symbol of the female deity. Scholars believe that the "Asherah poles" described in Scripture were actually huge phallic symbols. It was closely aligned with their worship of sex. Now note verses four and five:

> And he built altars in the house of the LORD, of which the LORD had
> said, "In Jerusalem I will put My name." For he built altars for all the
> host of heaven in the two courts of the house of the LORD.

I want you to catch the enormity of what is happening here. Solomon had built the temple in Jerusalem so that God might have a place where His presence could dwell and the people could come and worship. Manasseh's heart had become so corrupt and callous that he actually went into that holy place and set up altars of worship for these repulsive, imported gods.

That was bad enough. But it gets worse. Verse six tells us:

> He made his son pass through the fire.

One of the trendy gods Manasseh imported was called Molech. At certain times in the Valley of Hinnom in Israel, they would set up a massive iron idol, not unlike the huge statues of Buddha you might see in the Far East.

Before the festival to this god began, the priests would bring wood and build a roaring fire in the hollowed out back of this idol. They would stoke the fire until the iron image became white hot. The hands of this god were stretched out in front of it, palms open, in a receiving position. And as the people worshiped and worked themselves into a frenzy, they would take their first-born sons, get as close as they could to the fiery idol, and toss the child to his death in those white hot hands. Can you believe this guy?

But we're not quite through with Manasseh's résumé yet. Verse six also tells us that he

> ...practiced witchcraft and used divination, and dealt with mediums
> and spiritists.

The original language gives the idea that he not only dealt with these masters of the occult, but he placed them in positions of leadership in the country. In essence, he named witches and warlocks to his cabinet. But he wasn't through yet. Verse seven says:

> Then he set the carved image of Asherah that he had made, in the
> house of which the LORD said to David and to his son Solomon, "In
> this house and in Jerusalem, which I have chosen from all the tribes of
> Israel, I will put My name forever."

He actually had the gall to take an Asherah—to drag this massive phallic symbol—and place it in the temple, where the Spirit of God dwelt. Do you see how far down the tubes this man had gone? Remember, this was a man with a godly heritage. *He knew better.* He had a godly dad by the name of Hezekiah who had taught him the truth. He knew that there was one God. And this One God's most unique and holy name was Yahweh. He'd heard from childhood the stories of Yahweh's greatness, holiness, and glory.

But he deliberately turned his back on the God of his father.

Now, God does not let this kind of thing go unchecked. We make choices and God responds. Fifty-five years may seem like a lot of rope to us, but eventually, Manasseh came to the end of that rope.

GOD'S RESPONSE

God had a clear word for the renegade king of Judah:

> Now the LORD spoke through His servants the prophets, saying,
> "Because Manasseh king of Judah has done these abominations, having
> done wickedly more than all the Amorites did who were before him,
> and has also made Judah sin with his idols; therefore thus says the
> LORD, the God of Israel, 'Behold, I am bringing such calamity on
> Jerusalem and Judah, that whoever hears of it, both his ears shall
> tingle. And I will stretch over Jerusalem the line of Samaria and the

plummet of the house of Ahab, and I will wipe Jerusalem as one wipes

a dish, wiping it and turning it upside down.'" (vv. 10–13)

In other words, judgment day had arrived. Did you catch the phrase in the opening sentence of the above verse? Manasseh *did more* than all the Amorites who were before him. The Amorites were part of the culture generally known as the Canaanites. Before, the Scripture said that Manasseh equaled their sin and perversion. Now, he had passed them. In fact, he had lapped them. This guy was doing stuff they never thought of doing. And he was doing it in God's special city, Jerusalem.

Whenever you and I deviate from God's best for us, He speaks to our hearts. He usually speaks quietly at first, in that distinctive "still, small voice." If we continue in our sin, He will often put some people around us who will carefully and lovingly challenge us about our sin—because they care so much about us. Once again, we have the option to listen or to harden our hearts and ignore the counsel.

Obviously, Manasseh wasn't open. He didn't want to hear what God had to say to him. But God spoke through the prophets and said:

I will stretch over Jerusalem the line of Samaria and the plummet of
the house of Ahab. (v. 13)

These are terms used by survey crews. When you have a hill and want to level it, you first call the surveyors in with their plummet, or level. So what is God saying in response to the great and tragic sin of Manasseh? *I'm going to come into Jerusalem, and I'm going to level it.* And just in case that metaphor didn't sink in, the Lord used another one:

I will wipe Jerusalem as one wipes a dish, wiping it and turning it
upside down. (v. 13)

When you dry the dishes, how do you do it? Usually, you take the dish in your hand, dry one side, then turn it over and dry the other, so that every bit of moisture is sponged away. God is saying, "That's what I'm going to do in response to the sin of Manasseh. I'm going to wipe Jerusalem clean." Verse sixteen tells us:

> Moreover, Manasseh shed very much innocent blood until he had
> filled Jerusalem from one end to another.

A well-known Christian tradition tells us it was Manasseh who took the prophet Isaiah, put him in a hollowed out log and sawed him in half (see Hebrews 11:37). Why would he do such a thing? Because he did not want to hear the voice of God, and he tried to silence Him.

Verses seventeen and eighteen record Manasseh's obituary:

> Now the rest of the acts of Manasseh and all that he did and his sin
> which he committed, are they not written in the Book of the
> Chronicles of the Kings of Judah? And Manasseh slept with his fathers
> and was buried in the garden of his own house, in the garden of Uzza,
> and Amon his son became king in his place.

Oscar Wilde, an Irish poet and dramatist of the late nineteenth century, was known for his keen wit and gifted prose. Yet he spent several of the last years of his life in jail on a sodomy charge. Looking back on his life, he wrote these words:

> The gods have given me almost everything, but I let myself be lured
> into long spells of senseless and sensual ease. Tired of being on the
> heights, I deliberately went to the depths in search of a new sensation.
> What paradox was to me in the sphere of thought, perversity became
> to me in the sphere of passion. I drew careless of the lives of other
> people. I took pleasure where it pleased me, and passed on. And I
> forgot that every little action of the common day makes or unmakes
> character. And that therefore, what one has done in the secret
> chamber, one has someday to cry aloud from the housetop. I ceased to

be lord over myself. I was no longer the captain of my soul, and I did
not know it. I allowed pleasure to dominate me, and I ended in
horrible disgrace.

That quote could have been attributed to Manasseh. When I first read this
biblical account of Manasseh a number of years ago, it greatly disturbed me, and
I'll tell you why. It didn't seem right to me that a man could live that kind of life,
rule with such perversion and terror for fifty-five years, and then just die peacefully of old age like some retired businessman in Florida. In other words, it
didn't seem right that Manasseh—who lived like hell and created a living hell
for God's people—should just die peacefully in luxury and comfort at a ripe old
age. Somehow, that doesn't square with my sense of justice.

If radio commentator Paul Harvey were writing this chapter on Manasseh, he
might say at this point: "And after this commercial word...the *rest* of the story!"

The rest of *this* story is recorded in 2 Chronicles 33.

And the LORD spoke to Manasseh and his people, but they paid no
attention. Therefore the LORD brought the commanders of the army of
the king of Assyria against them, and they captured Manasseh with
hooks, bound him with bronze chains, and took him to Babylon.
(vv. 10–11)

Whoa! So old Manasseh didn't retire in Florida and sip piña coladas all day
by the pool after all! Just like Paul Harvey, Chronicles supplies the rest of the
story, and it's a doozy.

God brought in a military power stronger than Manasseh. They overwhelmed
the city, put chains on Manasseh's feet, jabbed a hook through his nose, and
hauled him in pain and humiliation to Babylon. When they got there, they tossed
him into a dungeon to let him rot.

End of the story? It would have been if *I* had been writing it. I would have
thrown away the key. He murdered the prophets, he sacrificed his baby son in

the fire, he led the people into witchcraft and Satanism, and he practiced sexual immorality in his own life and encouraged the nation to do the same. This guy deserved everything the Assyrians could dish out. But God allowed a very different ending. Note the next two verses:

And when he was in distress...

The Hebrew says literally, "when he was hemmed in the dungeon."

he entreated the LORD his God and humbled himself greatly before the God of his fathers. When he prayed to Him, He was moved by his entreaty and heard his supplication, and brought him again to Jerusalem to his kingdom. Then Manasseh knew that the LORD was God.

THAT is the rest of the story. And do you know what? I never liked that ending.

I didn't like it because I didn't like Manasseh. I didn't like the kind of things Manasseh did, and I didn't want him to get off easy and enjoy God's grace. But in case you haven't noticed by now, God isn't like you and me. He is radically different from what we are like.

It blows me away that God would do this for a jerk like Manasseh. It boggles my mind to think of the scope of this man's depravity. The people he killed! The families he destroyed! The judgment he brought on his whole country! And then he gets hemmed in, starts feeling bad, and he repents. And God *forgives* him. Just like that! And not only does He forgive him, but He gives him back his throne! Manasseh is set free and goes back to Jerusalem to become king again!

Do you remember the prophet Jonah? He went to preach judgment to the scumbag Ninevites, and then was absolutely *furious* because they believed God's message and repented. Why was he so angry? Because God had the nerve to hear the prayer of those despicable people and forgive them! History tells us Nineveh's judgment was put off for another 150 years. Jonah was so fried over God's grace toward those undeserving wretches that he asked the Lord to kill him. He figured he'd be better off dead than alive in a world with forgiven Ninevites.

That's about the way I reacted when I read about Manasseh. And do you know why I felt that way? It's because I really didn't appreciate just how close to Manasseh I really am. You see, my heart is made out of the same material as Manasseh's. This human heart of mine is just as corrupt as his was…and so is yours. Maybe we haven't sinned to the same degree, but trust me on this…we're made of the exact same stuff. And don't kid yourself; except for the grace of God, we have the potential to do precisely what he did.

Since I've reconsidered those sobering facts, a couple of principles have surfaced out of this man's strange life.

PRINCIPLE #1: GENUINE REPENTANCE UNLOCKS THE DOOR OF GOD'S MERCY

After careful research, I've determined that there are two kinds of repentance in the world.

Real and fake.

When Joshua, our youngest child, was two years old, he still didn't know very many words. But a couple of the first words he *did* learn were, "I'm torry! I'm torry!"

He meant, of course, that he was sorry. I'd walk into a room where he had created some kind of unbelievable havoc, and the first words out of his mouth were, "I'm torry, Daddy, I'm torry!"

But you know what? He really wasn't torry! He was only torry he got caught. Now that's not genuine repentance. True repentance comes from the heart. Genuine repentance is always accompanied with great remorse. It's an attitude that says, "If I had this to do over again, I wouldn't do it. I wish I could go back and change it, but I can't."

Let me tell you what genuine repentance is like. Have you ever had the dry heaves? That's genuine repentance. The great old Puritan Thomas Watson said that "repentance is the vomiting of the soul." It means that from your gut you abhor what you did and if given the opportunity to do it again, you wouldn't.

It means that you are repulsed by your sin and that you are sick of your sin. And you want nothing to do with it anymore. In the pit of your gut, you want nothing more than to change and be a different kind of man. And not only that, but you are going to demonstrate your change of heart by a change in your behavior. That's repentance. Genuine repentance.

You and I can't always tell the difference between genuine and artificial repentance. We're just as likely to fall for phony repentance and turn away in cynical disgust from the real thing. But God always knows the difference. And when Manasseh was sobbing convulsively in that Babylonian dungeon over his sin and was vomiting and repudiating the wickedness he had done, that's when God saw his heart and knew it was the real thing. Manasseh called out to God from his gut, and God listened.

Genuine repentance always brings evidence with it. That's how you recognize it. When John the Baptist preached, he said, "Bring forth fruit in keeping with your repentance." In other words, *demonstrate* your repentance. If you tell me that tree is an apple tree, then show me some apples. Those apples should be hanging all over that tree. Otherwise, how do I know it's an apple tree? That's what John the Baptist was trying to get across to those guys. And that's what Manasseh did after he was restored to the kingdom. He showed his fruit as he went about undoing the evil that he spent so many years doing.

> Now after this he built the outer wall of the city of David on the west
> side of Gihon. (v. 14)

That's where they were attacked by the Assyrians, so he rebuilt the weak place to keep them out. Note verses fifteen and sixteen:

> He also removed the foreign gods and the idol from the house of the
> LORD, as well as all the altars which he had built on the mountain of
> the house of the LORD and in Jerusalem, and he threw them outside
> the city. And he set up the altar of the LORD and sacrificed peace

> offerings and thank offerings on it; and he ordered Judah to serve the
> LORD God of Israel.

That's repentance. That's the authentic article. And genuine repentance—whether it is in the life of Manasseh or Steve Farrar or you—unlocks the floodgates of God's amazing mercy and forgiveness. But there's a second principle that I learned from this account.

PRINCIPLE #2: MY PAST LIFE DOES NOT EXCLUDE ME FROM PRESENT SERVICE

My brother Jeff pastors Central Peninsula Church in Foster City, California. Foster City is a suburb of San Francisco—not exactly the Bible belt. Jeff got the idea several years ago of starting a Friday night service because there are so many people in the Bay Area who are in Alcoholics Anonymous or other support groups, and Friday night is the toughest night of the week for them. Friday night is the night they used to kick off the weekend. But now they're trying to get off alcohol and drugs.

They call the service Higher Power. And Jesus Christ is the Higher Power. Now this service would probably break all of your categories. The music is provided by a band made up of former professional musicians who've given their lives to Christ. They can still boogie, but now they do it for Jesus. And Jeff, who has this uncanny ability to relate the gospel to people who don't come out of a church culture, gets up and teaches from the Scriptures. He's got 'em laughing and he's got 'em crying as he teaches the Truth.

The building is jammed every Friday night. There are people there who are heroin addicts, people who have records longer than your arm, and people who have lived immoral lifestyles and have AIDS. Now, wouldn't you agree that those people need to know Jesus Christ? Sure you would. And that's exactly what is happening.

What's really amazing is that Jeff has taken some of these guys and over the years discipled them. And now these same men have become strong leaders.

Jeff's top three *leaders* have a combined total of forty-five years in federal pen-
itentiaries. These are guys who've been involved in everything from running
arms to Colombian drug dealers, to armed robbery, to you name it. When Jeff
is out of town, the guy teaching the Scriptures so effectively in his place will
usually be someone who did significant time at San Quentin or Huntsville. If
you had thought of messing with some of these guys ten years ago, they
wouldn't have thought twice about sticking you. But now the only blade they
use is the one that is "living and active and sharper than any two-edged sword."

You see, just like Manasseh, these men had their old life. But now, because
of what Jesus Christ has done in their hearts, they have new life. *And they are
being used by Him.* Most of them had a lousy start. In fact, they didn't even get
into the race 'til later in life. Shoot, they didn't even know that there *was* a race.
But let me tell you something about these guys. They're going to finish strong.
Just like Manasseh did.

How do I know they're going to finish strong? They've all have had serious cases of the dry heaves. They've rejected and vomited their old way of
living. They abhor what they did and never want to go back. They are repulsed
by the thought of turning back to their former manner of living. These guys
want to know Christ and they want to obey Him. They've repented. And they
are being used.

It sounds to me like what Paul said to the church at Corinth.

> Or do you not know that the unrighteous shall not inherit the
> kingdom of God? Do not be deceived; neither fornicators, nor
> idolaters, nor adulterers, nor effeminate by perversion, nor homo-
> sexuals, nor thieves, nor the covetous, nor drunkards, nor revilers, nor
> swindlers, shall inherit the kingdom of God. *And such were some of you;*
> but you were washed, but you were sanctified, but you were justified
> in the name of the Lord Jesus Christ, and in the Spirit of our God.
> (1 Corinthians 6:9–11)

Manasseh would have fit right in on Friday nights at Higher Power. Who knows? He might even have played keyboard on "Amazing Grace." Because if anyone could ever sing with his whole heart about the grace that is amazing, it would be Manasseh.

DEALING WITH OLD MEMORIES

Tell me something. Do you think that Manasseh ever woke up in the middle of the night in a cold sweat, dreaming of all the wrong he'd done? Do you think he was ever troubled by dark memories and deep regret? *After* Manasseh was forgiven, after he had humbled himself, received the forgiveness of God, and was restored to his kingdom, do you think he ever had moments when he condemned himself for his past sin? Do you think he ever grieved over the sacrifice of his baby son to that fire god? Do you think he ever sorrowed over the innocent men he killed? Do you think he ever had trouble sleeping at night because of the multitudes he'd led into immorality? Do you think he was ever haunted by his past, *after* he was forgiven?

If he was a human being, the answer has to be yes. In spite of his forgiveness and restoration, Manasseh must have wrestled with terrible feelings of guilt *after* he was forgiven.

Whenever I think about guilt, I think about something I once heard about circus elephants.

When the elephants are just babies, the trainer puts a shackle around one of their legs, with a chain attached to a stake. These babies are maybe three to four hundred pounds at best, and they will try and try to get away from that chain. But they can't.

But the strange thing is that massive adult elephants—which may weigh a couple of tons apiece—can be held by the very same shackle as the one used on the youngsters.

How is this possible? Number one, elephants really do have great memories.

But number two, they aren't all that bright. The adult elephant remembers how he was staked up as a baby and couldn't get away from the stake. And at a certain point, as a baby, he became convinced that he could never get away. So now as an adult, he doesn't even try. That elephant is not chained to the stake; he's chained to the idea that he can never get away. That's how a ten-pound stake can hold down a two-ton elephant.

Some of us have found ourselves tied to our past just like a circus elephant chained to a stake. This is one of the primary tools and schemes of the enemy to defeat Christians and to keep us from finishing strong. What does the enemy do? He simply mines the shadowy depths of our memory. He throws our past back at us. It may be one major sin from years past, and we still grieve over it and deeply regret it. Yes, we've been forgiven. Yes, we belong to Jesus Christ, but that failure keeps drifting back into our minds like a dark, paralyzing fog whenever we seek to move out and do something significant for the Lord. We're like that elephant chained to the stake. That big old critter isn't physically restricted by that stake at all. He has the strength and resources to yank that thing out of the ground as if it were a toothpick. Yet the elephant remains chained by its memory. And so are many of us.

Maybe it was sexual immorality. Or lying to get your job. Or cruelty. Or neglect. Or a broken vow or pledge to God. Whatever it was, the enemy keeps throwing that one sin up in your face. The enemy uses it to paralyze you, intimidate you, and neutralize you. No, Satan cannot take away your salvation. But he can rob you of your joy. And all he has to do is bring up that one past sin.

Sir Arthur Conan Doyle, the creator of master detective Sherlock Holmes, was a great practical joker. In one of his more fiendish pranks, he sent out identical telegrams to twelve of his friends. The telegrams were anonymous and simply said: "All has been discovered. Flee at once." What's funny is that within twenty-four hours, all twelve men had fled the country.

We all have skeletons in the closet. We all have things in our past that embarrass us and shame us. As a result, some of us are chained to the past today.

And it's hard to run a race when you're pulling that kind of chain. You're going to need some strong help to cut through those rusty old links.

THE JAWS OF LIFE

Have you ever heard of the Jaws of Life? Whenever there's a terrible car accident and someone is trapped inside, the fire and rescue crews will soon arrive with the Jaws of Life. These things can cut through anything: steel, brick, metal, and the twisted chassis and body of a car that's been hit head-on by an eighteen wheeler.

Friend, it's time to call for the Jaws of Life. It's time to cut through the chain of past sin and guilt that is holding you back and keeping you from finishing strong.

We need the Jaws of Life to cut us free from biblical ignorance.

If I were politically correct, I probably wouldn't say anyone was ignorant; I would say he was "theologically challenged."

But the fact remains that many Christians don't understand what Scripture teaches about forgiveness. I can say this because for a number of years I was ignorant, too—chained like an obedient elephant to my past. There were a couple of things I had done as a younger man that absolutely humiliated me. Every time I wanted to do something for the Lord, those old sins would rise up and slap me down, squashing my spirit flat as roadkill on the interstate.

The enemy would continually bring these up before me, and I felt like I couldn't be used by God. I was a Christian, I'd been forgiven, but I was ignorant of what Jesus had really accomplished for me on the cross. I only partially understood it.

In John 19:29, Jesus made this triumphant statement from the cross: *"It is finished."*

For years, I never understand what He meant. *What* was finished? It was the work His Father had sent Him to accomplish. He was the Lamb of God who took away the sins of the world. And when Jesus was on the cross—at that particular point in history—He paid for my sin. In 1 John 2:2, it says that He died not only for my sins, but also for the sins of the entire world. At that moment on Calvary, your sins and my sins—ALL our sins—were paid for.

Interestingly enough, the Greek word translated "It is finished" can also be translated "Paid in full." For you see, that's what happens when a debt is paid in full. It is finished. I like the chorus that says:

> I owed a debt I could not pay,
> He paid a debt He did not owe.

That's it. That's the gospel. You owed a debt of sin that you could never hope to cover with your personal check. So Jesus paid the debt He did not owe. And that was your debt. And it was my debt. In other words, He's got us covered.

There are many denominations that believe the Bible but don't teach much about the fullness of grace. I was raised in such a church. They were wonderful, godly folks who loved Jesus Christ, but they were honestly ignorant of what Jesus accomplished at the cross.

Tell me: when Jesus died on the cross, how many of your sins were future? The obvious answer is *all* of them. Because when Jesus died on the cross, *you* were future—and so was I. Scripture tells us that in that one act, He died for the sins of the entire world. He died for my sins. He died for my children's sins. And He died for the sins of *their* children—who aren't even in existence yet. He paid for their sin. And He has paid for every sin I will ever commit for the rest of my life.

Psalm 103:10 reads:

> He has not dealt with us according to our sins,
> nor rewarded us according to our iniquities.

Let me ask you a question. Did He deal with Manasseh according to his sins? Did Manasseh deserve to be restored to his kingdom? No, God did not deal with this man according to his sins; if He had, Manasseh would have been vaporized a long time before. He doesn't deal with me according to my sin, either. He doesn't deal with you according to your sin. And He doesn't reward us according to our iniquities. If He did, there would be no reward.

No, He rewards us according to grace. He did that with Manasseh, He does it with you, and He does it with me. I didn't understand this; I was ignorant of it.

> For as high as the heavens are above the earth, so great is His loving-
> kindness to those who fear Him. As far as the east is from the west, so
> far has He removed our transgressions from us. (Psalm 103:11–12)

And how far is that? Well, it's farther than you and I can imagine. And that's how far the Bible says He has removed our transgressions from us. Whether we realize it or not or appreciate it or not, *they're gone.*

We need the Jaws of Life to cut us free from unbelief.

Perhaps your problem isn't ignorance; perhaps it's plain old unbelief. "But wait a minute," you say. "I'm a Christian. I believe in Jesus Christ. How can I be troubled with unbelief?"

Yet we do struggle with unbelief as Christian men, don't we? Sometimes the risen Lord needs to speak the same word to us that He spoke to those down-hearted, doubting disciples on the road to Emmaus: "O foolish men and slow of heart to believe!" (Luke 24:25).

When it comes right down to it, some of us have trouble really *believing* in the extent of Christ's work for us on the cross. We're slow and strangely reluctant to believe in the liberating truth of 1 John 1:9:

> If we confess our sins, He is faithful and righteous to forgive us our
> sins and to cleanse us from all unrighteousness.

Martin Luther used to spend hours and hours in a confessional box. He would spend six to eight hours confessing his sins to a priest. Then he would walk out and immediately be haunted by something he had forgotten to confess. Some people still do that today.

If you're still struggling with the chains of guilt, you have not believed what Jesus Christ said in His Word.

In his book *Will Daylight Come?* Robert Heffler pens this moving illustration:

> There was a little boy visiting his grandparents on their farm. And he was given a slingshot to play with out in the woods. He practiced in the woods but he could never hit the target. And getting a little discouraged, he headed back to dinner. As he was walking back he saw Grandma's pet duck. Just out of impulse, he let fly, hit the duck square in the head, and killed it. He was shocked and grieved. In a panic, he hid the dead duck in the wood pile...only to see his sister watching. Sally had seen it all, but she said nothing.
>
> After lunch that day grandma said, "Sally, let's wash the dishes." But Sally said, "Grandma, Johnny told me he wanted to help in the kitchen today, *didn't you Johnny?*" And then she whispered to him, "Remember, the duck?"
>
> So Johnny did the dishes.
>
> Later Grandpa asked if the children wanted to go fishing, and Grandma said, "I'm sorry but I need Sally to help make supper." But Sally smiled and said, "Well, that's all right because Johnny told me he wanted to help." And she whispered again, "Remember, the duck?" So Sally went fishing and Johnny stayed.
>
> After several days of Johnny doing both his chores and Sally's, he finally couldn't stand it any longer. He came to Grandma and confessed that he killed the duck. She knelt down, gave him a hug, and said, "Sweetheart, I know. You see, I was standing at the window and I saw the whole thing. But because I love you, I forgave you. But I was just wondering how long you would let Sally make a slave of you."

I don't know what's in your past. I don't know what one sin the enemy keeps throwing up in your face. But whatever it is, I want you to know something.

Jesus Christ was standing at the window. And He saw the whole thing. But because He loves you, He has forgiven you. Perhaps He's wondering how long you'll let the enemy make a slave out of you.

Do you know what the name Manasseh means in Hebrew? It means "forgotten." And that's exactly what Jesus has done with our sin, according to Hebrews 10:17. He's *forgotten* it. The great thing about God is that He not only forgives, but He forgets. He says:

> And their sins and their lawless deeds, I will remember no more.

He's not remembering it, so why are you remembering it? The next time the enemy throws up that one sin in your face, tell him to take a long walk off a short pier.

And tell him to take that chain with him.

CHAPTER EIGHT

FAILURE THAT EQUIPS YOU TO FINISH *

He who has never failed cannot be great.
Failure is the true test of greatness.

HERMAN MELVILLE

Reed Joseph was adopted as an infant into one of the wealthiest families in America. He went to a very exclusive prep school in upstate New York, then headed west after graduation to play football at Stanford. Upon graduation from Stanford, Joseph immediately enlisted in the military. He spent the majority of World War II making bombing runs over Germany and returned home a highly decorated military hero. He then picked up an M.B.A. at Harvard and a Ph.D. at Yale.

Reed Joseph was a success. He was the last guy you'd expect to be wanted for manslaughter. But that's exactly the charge that would change his life and end his career. You should know that the following account is not a piece of carefully crafted fiction. It really happened.

In his early thirties, Joseph decided to make a run at politics. He decided to go for broke and run for the United States Senate. He won. Thirty-three years old and a United States senator. Once again, his string of successes continued.

* This chapter appeared previously in a work no longer available.

153

But it all changed when he got on the subway.

After enjoying the premiere of a new play on Broadway, he and his wife decided to do something they hadn't done in years. Just for fun, they would take the subway back to their hotel. Little did he know as he descended the stairway to the train that in just a few minutes his life would be changed forever.

He heard the screams as they were running to catch the waiting train. He turned and saw an elderly Hasidic Jew, wearing the traditional black suit and hat you see so often in New York, being beaten by a guy who had to be at least 6'6" and three hundred pounds. The old man's face was gushing blood from the relentless blows. In a flash, the senator bolted toward the assailant and brought him down with the form that had made him an all-American twenty years prior.

Quickly the assailant was on his feet, now charging him with a hideous looking pipe in his hand. It was instinct, sheer instinct, that came out of his military training that put the man on his back. And it took only one survival-training blow to the throat. The attacker collapsed in the fetal position, gasping for air that wouldn't come. Within seconds, he was dead.

And so was the senator's career. He was forty years old, and he was finished.

This is a true story. It really happened. Except for the fact that this guy's real name was not Reed Joseph. And he wasn't an American. He didn't go to Stanford, didn't fly bombers over Germany, didn't run for the senate, and he never took the subway.

But other than that, it's a true story.

Except that his name wasn't Reed. But he *was* adopted. They could have called him Reed, because they found him among some reeds along the riverbank. But they didn't. They called him Moses.

His last name wasn't Joseph but it *could* have been, for he was a descendant of Joseph, the great Israeli prime minister of Egypt. That's why his Jewish family was in Egypt.

F. B. Meyer gives some valuable historical information on Moses' life not commonly known:

Moses was brought up in the palace, and he was treated as the grandson of Pharaoh. When he was old enough he was probably sent to be educated in the college which had grown up around the Temple of the Sun, and has been called "the Oxford of Ancient Egypt."...
Stephen says: "Moses was learned in all the wisdom of the Egyptians" (Acts 7:22).

But Moses was something more than a royal student: he was a statesman and a soldier. Stephen tells us that he was "mighty in words and deeds": mighty in words—there is the statesman; mighty in deeds—there is the soldier. [The Jewish historian] Josephus says that while he was still in his early manhood the Ethiopians invaded Egypt, routed the army sent against them, and threatened Memphis.

In the panic the oracles were consulted, and on their recommendation Moses was entrusted with the command of the royal troops. He immediately took the field, surprised and defeated the enemy, and captured their principal city...and returned to Egypt laden with the spoils of victory."[1]

The facts of the story are these:

- Moses was adopted into the wealthiest family in Egypt.
- Moses was educated in "all the wisdom of the Egyptians." He went to the very best schools and had the equivalent of an M.B.A. and Ph.D.
- Moses was a highly decorated military leader.
- Moses, by virtue of his military leadership and his membership in the house of Pharaoh, was a logical choice to perhaps one day be Pharaoh himself.
- Moses saw one of his Hebrew brothers being beaten by a taskmaster, went to his aid, and killed the guard.

Something about this story of Moses has a contemporary feel to it. Many people today are devoting their lives to reaching the top of the pyramid. Moses was in line to *own* the pyramids. But Moses made a very costly mistake. With one impulsive act, Moses fell off the pyramid. Now he could *never* finish strong. Or so he thought.

At age thirty-nine, Moses had it all. Power, prestige, education, wealth, and a career with unbelievable potential. By anyone's standards, Moses was successful.

When we think of Moses, we tend to think of the plagues, the Red Sea, and all the other miraculous things God did for Israel under his leadership. Those events transpired in the last forty years of his life. But we tend to overlook his early years. We can't afford to do that, because it is the study of his early years that yields tremendous insights into how God will often work in our own lives—and help us hit that tape at life's finish line.

God called Moses at the age of forty to go back to school. Now Moses didn't know this at the time. He thought he'd completed his education. He had an Egyptian B.A., M.B.A., and Ph.D. But there was one degree that he was lacking.

Moses needed to get an M.C.A.

THE TOUGHEST DEGREE OF ALL

An M.C.A. is a Masters in Character Acquisition. And for what God had planned for Moses, getting that degree wasn't optional. It was mandatory.

The M.C.A. is not an easy degree. That's why very few people sign up for it on their own. It usually takes a radical, unforeseen series of events in their lives to get them into the program. Events like bankruptcy, divorce, moral failure, cocaine or alcohol abuse, or a major career setback to name just a few. The program only consists of four core courses and a few electives (that God selects), but it took Moses nearly forty years to graduate. The Masters of Character Acquisition is a very tough program. And God is still signing people up today for the program. In fact, some of you may be *in* it and not even realize it.

But we're getting ahead of ourselves.

Moses lived to be one hundred and twenty years old. His life can be divided into three chapters of forty years each:

- The first forty years he was an unqualified success.
- The middle forty years he was an undisputed failure.
- The last forty years he was finally fit for the Master's use.

Moses knew in his heart of hearts that he was not in those privileged circumstances by chance. He knew he was there for a reason. God had reached down and taken him from a family of slaves into the very family of Pharaoh. And God had a purpose in doing so.

Stephen gives us particular insight into what was going on in Moses' mind when he moved to defend his Jewish brother. Apparently, there was more on Moses' mind than just defending a helpless slave.

> And when he saw one of them being treated unjustly, he defended
> him and took vengeance for the oppressed by striking down the
> Egyptian. And he supposed that his brethren understood that God was
> granting them deliverance through him; but they did not understand.
> (Acts 7:24–25)

Verse twenty-five makes it very clear that right around the age of forty, Moses knew he had been chosen by God to be the deliverer of Israel. He was dead right about the task, but dead wrong about the timing. As a result of his forty-year miscalculation, note what happened:

> And on the following day he appeared to them as they were fighting
> together, and he tried to reconcile them in peace, saying, "Men, you
> are brethren, why do you injure one another?" But the one who was
> injuring his neighbor pushed him away, saying, "Who made you a
> ruler and judge over us? You do not mean to kill me as you killed the
> Egyptian yesterday, do you?" And at this remark Moses fled, and
> became an alien in the land of Midian. (Acts 7:26–29)

Around the age of forty, Moses instituted his own plan to bring about the Exodus. And it didn't work.

This event gives us some clues about the kind of man Moses was. Stop for a minute and think about what he was trying to pull off. His goal was to take two million slave laborers, plus women and children, out of Egypt and back to the land of their fathers. These people were the economic backbone of Egypt. Yet Moses believed they would follow his leadership, revolt against Egypt, and find their freedom. It takes a special kind of man to attempt this kind of rebellion.

- He must have had great self-esteem.
- He must have had great self-confidence.
- He must have had great courage.

Moses believed in himself. He knew he was gifted and well connected. And he knew he had what it would take to pull off the Exodus. He knew it because he had succeeded in everything he had undertaken up to that point in his life. That's why he fully expected to be successful in this venture as well.

Moses was a mover and shaker. A leader with a capital "L." Except this time. This time he hit a brick wall.

The account recorded in Exodus gives us another angle on the events Stephen alluded to.

> Now it came about in those days, when Moses had grown up, that he went out to his brethren and looked on their hard labors; and he saw an Egyptian beating a Hebrew, one of his brethren. So he looked this way and that, and when he saw there was no one around, he struck down the Egyptian and hid him in the sand....When Pharaoh heard of this matter, he tried to kill Moses. But Moses fled from the presence of Pharaoh and settled in the land of Midian; and he sat down by a well. (Exodus 2:11–12, 15)

Notice one fatal flaw in this account. As Moses contemplated going to the aid of his Hebrew brother, Scripture says that "he looked this way and that." In other words, he looked around to his left and then to his right.

But do you know what he failed to do? He never looked *up*.

There is a type of self-confidence and self-esteem that is healthy and good. But there is an excessive self-confidence that is very harmful to one's spiritual health. How do you tell the difference between the two? Easy. A wrong self-confidence is usually characterized by prayerlessness. We're so busy instituting our plan and following our instincts and leading, and we are so confident it will all work out as we have planned, that we never bother to look up. It's not that we are going against God, it's just that we don't have a sense that we really need to depend on Him. We think we can handle things without bothering the Lord.

In John 15:5 Jesus said, "I am the vine, you are the branches; he who abides in Me, and I in him, he bears much fruit; for apart from Me *you can do nothing.*" The person with excessive self-confidence really doesn't believe that last phrase. He may believe it intellectually, but he doesn't believe it experientially. That's exactly where Moses was.

This is why Moses' failure had to be particularly bitter. He knew God had placed him in a position of power and authority to secure the release of the children of Israel. And he had blown it. And worse still, he was the only one on the horizon who could have possibly helped Israel. There were no other Hebrews in positions of power or influence like him. He was it. Or rather, he *used* to be it. His golden opportunity and his people's one shot at freedom was over.

Moses experienced the original mid-life crisis. Around the age of forty, he went

- from the palace to the pasture
- from success to failure
- from wealth to poverty
- from significance to insignificance
- from privilege to persecution
- from freedom to felon
- from a purpose in life to no purpose whatsoever
- from a great future to a grim future

May I remind you that all of that happened literally *overnight.* You've heard of an overnight success. Moses was an overnight failure. He lost it all in just twenty-four little hours. That's what you call major league mid-life crisis.

Many men experience some type of transition around the age of forty. Midlife is when men are forced to come to grips with the changes that have occurred in their lives. Consider the changes that Moses faced at the age of forty.

- *Moses had a change of address.*

He went from the palace of Pharaoh to the pastures of Midian. That's like going from the White House to running a gas station in the middle of the Mojave Desert. There were no Hiltons or Marriotts in Midian. It seemed God-forsaken territory.

- *Moses had a change of vocation.*

Moses was a leader of men. Now he was a leader of sheep. Just stop for a minute and think of the psychological and emotional trauma that Moses had to have experienced with such a traumatic change in his life. This guy wasn't cut out to lead sheep. This guy could lead a nation. But there he was in the middle of a desert, playing den mother to a flock of woollies.

Most men get their self-worth from what they do. Moses wasn't doing anything...except trying to find enough grass and water to keep those sheep alive. I think he must have experienced a tremendous personal identity crisis during those years, don't you?

- *Moses had a change of status.*

Earlier in this book we talked about cultural success being an elevation in privilege, power, and wealth. Moses had all of those things and then he lost them. And he didn't lose them gradually.

That makes me think that Moses must have struggled with depression. Generally speaking, depression stems from some type of loss (unless of course, the depression is the result of some kind of chemical imbalance). Whether it is losing a spouse, losing a job, losing a sense of identity or self-worth—whatever the loss is—it can bring depression. Depression was bound to follow. This guy may have been an extremely talented man, but he was still very human.

Emotional rejection can hit us at any time in life. Moses had been rejected by Pharaoh. At least that made some sense. But what didn't make sense was the rejection by his own people! It always hurts worse when the rejection comes from inside our own camp. It might be from a friend, a loyal coworker, a spouse, or some other person whom we trusted. That's why the wound is so deep. We thought they were on our team, and they rejected us.

After leading Britain to victory against Nazi Germany, Winston Churchill earned his place in history. Britain had been so intimidated by Hitler that petitions were being circulated at Oxford and Cambridge that Britain should surrender to Germany. Hitler was roving across Europe at will. His war machine was seemingly unstoppable. Most of Britain was defeated psychologically before the war ever started. But then Winston Churchill took charge as prime minister on May 10, 1940. One month later, leaders from around the world were wondering whether, if France was defeated, Britain would quit as well. To counteract this notion, Churchill took to the airwaves over BBC radio:

> Upon this battle depends the survival of Christian civilization.
>> Upon it depends our own British life,
>>> and the long continuity of our institutions and our Empire....
> Hitler knows that he will have to break us on this island
>> or lose the war.
> If we can stand up to him all Europe may be free
>> and the life of the world may move forward
>>> into broad, sunlit uplands.
> But if we fail, then the whole world,
>> including the United States,
>>> including all we have known and cared for,

Will sink into the abyss of a new Dark Age

    made more sinister, and perhaps more protracted,

        by the lights of perverted science.

Let us therefore brace ourselves to our duties,

    and so bear ourselves

        that if the British Empire and its Commonwealth

    last for a thousand years,

Men will say:

    "This was their finest hour."[2]

By the power of his will and personality, Churchill, as one historian put it, "transformed cowards into brave men."[3] And the incredible began to happen. Britain actually began believing they could not only survive but actually prevail!

Five years later, the incredible became a reality. On May 7, 1945, Germany surrendered to the Allied forces. How did Britain show their thanks to the man who had singlehandedly restored their resolve and determination? On July 25, not quite three months after Germany's defeat, the nation showed their thanks to this great man by summarily voting him out of office.

Churchill was rejected by the very people he had helped to save! He had pulled them together as a nation, and then with victory in hand, they turned on him. When his wife told him that defeat may in fact be a blessing in disguise, Churchill responded: "If it is, then it is very effectively disguised."

That's how Moses felt. He could see no blessing in his circumstances. He could see *nothing* positive about his new position in life. And from a human perspective he was right.

Moses was wounded, Churchill was wounded, and perhaps you are wounded. Maybe you have experienced a setback that has sent you reeling. You may be feeling that there is no recovery from your circumstances. But that's not the case. The God who oversees and controls the events of history is overseeing your life as well. And He knows exactly what He is doing. You may have lost control of your circumstances, but He has not. Trust me, my friend. He has enrolled you in a course you didn't sign up for. And if you remain teachable, He'll make sure you finish strong.

THE MASTERS OF CHARACTER ACQUISITION

God was far from finished with Moses. Although Moses felt God had removed His hand from him, nothing was further from the truth. God's hand was as firmly on Moses in the desert as it had been when he was a babe in the bulrushes.

God was signing Moses up for a master's degree with a major in character development. While he was in the desert over the next forty years, Moses took four core courses:

1. Unemployment 101
2. Advanced Obscurity
3. Remedial Waiting
4. Intermediate Loneliness

Let's look at each of these courses, because God is still enrolling men and women today in this same curriculum.

COURSE #1—UNEMPLOYMENT 101

Moses was a scholar, statesman, and soldier. Those kinds of guys usually aren't looking in the classifieds for a job. With those kinds of credentials, jobs usually come looking for you. When you have that kind of track record, it seems that every other call you get is from a headhunter, looking to see if you would be interested in a more "lucrative" position.

Moses had always been a success. Just think of his situation. Because of his position and accomplishments, it's safe to surmise he was rather well off financially. He may have had a classy home near the country club that overlooked a gorgeous fairway. I imagine that he could afford to go to Vail or Jackson Hole for a week or two to do a little skiing. He possibly leased a German-made chariot every three years or so. I presume that his financial portfolio was adequately impressive. Let's put it this way: Moses probably didn't have to buy his Twinkies with food stamps. Unless I miss my guess, this guy was set financially.

It's hard for a guy like that to be unemployed. But that's exactly what he was. It probably took a week or two for the reality to set in, but eventually it did. The Golden Boy was out of a job. This was no lateral move, it was a permanent setback.

It's easy for us to read this stuff in the Bible and kind of blow right by it. But we can't do that. This guy was stunned. He was hurt, wounded, embarrassed, and humiliated. Unemployment 101 is a very tough course to take.

God is still enrolling his men in Unemployment 101. In the last six months, I've heard of two Christian executives, in cities two thousand miles apart, who have had similar experiences. These two men are not acquainted with one another, but there is an amazing similarity to their circumstances. Each received an exceptional offer from another firm. Both talked with their superiors candidly about their futures. Both received assurances they were safe from any future cutbacks; they were valued and secure members of the team. As a result both men turned down their respective offers. And within six weeks, both executives received their walking papers from the firms that were so "committed" to them.

Unemployment 101 inevitably attacks a man's self-worth. I certainly struggled with those feelings when I found myself unexpectedly enrolled in this course.

For nearly a year I was out of ministry. My time in Unemployment 101 came between my first and second pastorates. During that time I interviewed with seven different churches, and every one of them turned me down. I couldn't believe it! Most churches, it seems, don't want to hire a "former pastor." They want to hire a *current* pastor.

That's why I eventually had to call a guy I used to drive a truck for when I was in college. Fortunately, it was close to Christmas and they needed some extra help. So there I was at the age of thirty-two, driving an air freight truck. That was the job I had *before* I went to seminary. Now don't get me wrong. Driving a truck is an honorable profession. But it wasn't the profession I'd felt called to give my life to.

That was a very hard time in my life. I felt like a failure. I was really hurting. That's what happens to most guys who are honest when they take Unemployment 101. Quite frankly, it was a time of suffering for me. I think that Moses suffered when he took this course, and I think the two men I mentioned have suffered as well. Maybe you're suffering because you are currently enrolled in Unemployment 101.

Here's the thing that causes that kind of suffering: you have no idea how long this course is going to last. In most courses, you know when the midterm and final exams are coming. And then the class will be over. In Unemployment 101, the professor does not hand out a syllabus signifying the dates of the class. And that's the source of your suffering. *How long is this going to go on?* you ask yourself time and time again.

Here's the good news about Unemployment 101. This challenging course will cause you to suffer, but it's the suffering that qualifies you for ministry. You may be thinking, "I'm not in full-time ministry!" You may have no desire to be in full-time ministry, but if you know Jesus Christ, then you are in the ministry. And it is suffering that will equip you for the unique task God has set aside specifically for you. He has not shelved you. He is simply retooling. And you are the tool.

COURSE #2—ADVANCED OBSCURITY

Moses had gone from being somebody to nobody. In the good old days, Moses couldn't walk the streets of Egypt without being recognized. He never had to wait for a table in a nice restaurant. People would notice him as he drove his chariot through the city. That's what makes me think that Moses was not just confident. He was overconfident. And there is one tried and tested remedy for overconfidence. It is obscurity.

Midian wasn't a bit like Egypt. There were no impressive cities or admiring groups of people. Midian was a flat, barren area covered mostly by sand, rocks, and a few shrubs. It's a place of extreme heat in the day and brutal cold in the night. It is rarely comfortable. That's why it's so obscure.

Moses didn't have a chariot and there weren't any restaurants or servants. Except for Moses. Now he was a servant. When he fled from Egypt for his life, he went to Midian and sat down by a well. Exodus picks up the account:

> Now the priest of Midian had seven daughters; and they came to draw water, and filled the troughs to water their father's flock. Then the shepherds came and drove them away, but Moses stood up and helped them, and watered their flock. When they came to Reuel their father, he said, "Why have you come back so soon today?" So they said, "An Egyptian delivered us from the hand of the shepherds; and what is more, he even drew the water for us and watered the flock." And he said to his daughters, "Where is he then? Why is it that you have left the man behind? Invite him to have something to eat." And Moses was willing to dwell with the man, and he gave his daughter Zipporah to Moses. Then she gave birth to a son, and he named him Gershom, for he said, "I have been a sojourner in a foreign land." (Exodus 2:16–22)

It's important that we understand that those six verses cover the entire middle *forty years* of Moses' life. That's it. Forty years get six verses. Why? Because Moses was obscure. Not much was happening. There really wasn't anything to report. It seemed as though God had forgotten about Moses. But He hadn't. In those forty years of obscurity, solitude, and quietness, God was at work. He was rebuilding His man from the inside out.

God is still enrolling his people in Advanced Obscurity. In our frantic pace to get our piece of the American Dream, we don't have time to go back to school for a course like this. That's why God has to step in and change our circumstances. Some type of struggle with obscurity is required if you are going to earn your M.C.A. Obscurity is tough, especially if you are in a hurry to climb the corporate ladder. But climbing the corporate ladder will never fit you to finish strong. God wants you to climb the *character* ladder.

John Luther wrote that "good character is more to be praised than outstanding talent. Most talents are, to some extent, a gift. Good character, by contrast, is not given to us. We have to build it piece by piece—by thought, choice, courage and determination." There is no better place to begin making those right choices than in the bleak, gray sands of obscurity.

It may be an obscure job that is obviously going nowhere; it may be an illness that suddenly knocked you off your feet and ripped you out of your normal routine. God always has a deeper purpose when He puts His people in this course of Advanced Obscurity. What is His purpose? You probably can't see it now. You'll have to wait. And if there's anything we hate to do, it's wait. Interestingly enough, that's why He signs us up for the next course.

COURSE #3—REMEDIAL WAITING

Moses was in a tremendous hurry to accomplish his timetable. After all, he was nearly forty! If he was going to accomplish his appointed purpose, then he needed to get with the program!

Peter Marshall once observed that "we are in such a hurry that we hate to miss one panel of a revolving door." I've got some bad news for you. You may be in hurry, but God is not in a hurry.

We are in such a hurry that many of us cannot imagine our lives without Federal Express. "When it absolutely, positively, has to be there overnight." I don't know what I would do without Federal Express. I probably average one or two late-night visits a week to my local FedEx office.

What in the world would we FedEx addicts have done one hundred years ago? Back then they didn't have Federal Express, they had Pony Express. I can see the commercials now. Pony Express: when it absolutely, positively, has to be there in three months. Can you imagine waiting three months for a package? We have trouble waiting three days.

The bad news is this: God rarely uses Federal Express to build character into our lives. He doesn't overnight or fax character to us. It takes time to build character. Lots of time. That's why He is taking so much time in your life. God isn't in a hurry.

Can you believe that God took *forty years* to build character into the life of Moses? That's how long it took Moses to earn his M.C.A. Most of us want character in forty minutes, and even that is pushing it.

It seems to me that God's motto is "When it absolutely, positively, has to be there in forty years." Moses was in a hurry to deliver his suffering countrymen. He was sure God had placed him in his unique position so that he could have a unique ministry. And he was right. But he overlooked one thing. God has a principle, and the principle is this: character development comes before ministry.

Let me ask you a question. When was the last time you stopped when you saw a yellow light? Most of us accelerate when we come to an intersection with a yellow light! Why? Yellow lights are indicators that we should prepare to stop. But we don't have time to stop for a minute or two. We're in a hurry.

That's why remedial waiting is such a difficult course for us. But it is absolutely necessary for the character remodeling that God is undertaking in our lives. Are you at a place in your life where you are tired of waiting? You may be waiting for a promotion, waiting to conceive a child, waiting for your business to turn around, waiting for employment, waiting for your house to sell, waiting for your child to finish those bone-marrow treatments, waiting for that depression to finally leave.

May I offer a word of encouragement here? You should know that you are right on schedule. Maybe not on your schedule, but on His schedule. He knows *precisely* what He is doing in your life. Every trial has a beginning, a middle, and an end. You cannot determine where you are in your trial, but He knows exactly where you are. And He is moving you along at just the right pace. Someone once said that everything is in walking distance, if you have enough time. Believe it or not, you've got time. You've got *plenty* of time, because you belong to Jesus Christ. And He literally has all the time in the world.

COURSE #4—INTERMEDIATE LONELINESS

Although Moses grew up in Pharaoh's palace, he was raised by his mother. God conveniently arranged for Pharaoh's daughter to hire Moses' mom to raise him. As I read between the lines, I think it's safe to surmise that Moses was not isolated from his family. Although he was a part of royalty, he was still able to enjoy contact with his mother, and I imagine to some degree with his father, brother, and sister. But the day he had to flee for his life all family ties were severed.

Loneliness is tough. It's tougher on us than most of us realize. Research has demonstrated that prolonged loneliness can even affect us physically.

- At Ohio State University College of Medicine, scientists found that patients who scored above average in loneliness had significantly poorer functioning of their immune systems.

- In Sweden, a ten-year study of 150 middle-aged men found that social isolation was one of the best predictors of mortality.

- A report published in the journal *Science* said that social isolation is as significant to mortality rates as smoking, high blood pressure, high cholesterol, obesity, and lack of physical exercise. In fact, when age is adjusted for, social isolation is as great or greater a mortality risk than smoking.

- At Stanford University School of Medicine, Dr. David Spiegel conducted research in which patients with metastatic breast cancer were randomly divided into two groups. One group received the usual medical care, while the other received the usual care plus weekly ninety-minute support group meetings for one year. Although he planned the study expecting there would be no difference in life span between the two groups, five years later he found that the patients who attended the weekly group support meetings had twice the survival rate of the other group.[4]

Most leaders like to be with people. They enjoy the company of their followers. But in the desert, Moses didn't have any followers. Well, he had a few sheep. But the fact is, Moses wasn't in the desert to lead; he was in the desert *to be led*. That's why he had to be isolated. God had to get him off by himself so that He could have his undivided attention. Moses thought he was a leader, but a leader really isn't a leader until he has learned to follow. God would not use Moses until Moses had learned to submit to God and to God's timetable. So Moses was alone.

In a period of twenty-four hours, Moses found himself isolated from every relationship that he ever enjoyed. There was no calling them from a phone booth as he was on the run. It was over. No time for explanations, no opportunity to say good-bye.

When God calls us to take Intermediate Loneliness, He doesn't usually completely cut us from all human relationships. Even though Moses had lost his family in Egypt, God gave him a wife in Midian, and before long he had two sons. But there was still a major void in Moses' life because of the relationships he could no longer enjoy.

Loneliness is never a pleasant experience. But God, in his wisdom, at times will separate us from our normal network of family and friends. Isolation is an opportunity to get to know Him better.

THE BOTTOM LINE

Moses must have felt like an absolute failure. He had lost his career, his status, his reputation, his family, his friends, and his future. If that had happened to you, wouldn't *you* feel like a failure? Of course, you would. Any human being would feel that way.

That's why some of you are struggling with failure right now. You have experienced some type of setback in your life, and you struggle with failure nearly every waking moment. It could have been a career setback, a relational setback, or some other type of major loss in your life. But the fact of the matter is this: you're in the desert just as Moses was in the desert.

You may not be wandering around on literal sand dunes looking for an iced tea, but you may be in a spiritual desert, an emotional desert, or a relational desert. And you feel like a failure. Well, you're not a failure. God has simply pulled you aside to take some courses. And those courses have to do with your character development. There is only one way to earn a Masters of Character Acquisition, and that is through hardship.

I like Miles Stanford's insight here: "Many believers are simply frantic over the fact of failure in their lives, and they will go to all lengths in trying to hide it, ignore it, or rationalize about it. And all the time they are resisting the main instrument in the Father's hand for conforming us to the image of His Son!"[5]

Henry Ward Beecher wrote: "It is defeat that turns bone to flint, and gristle to muscle, and makes people invincible, and forms those heroic natures that are now in ascendancy in the world. Do not, then, be afraid of defeat. You are never so near to victory as when defeated in a good cause."

Everyone fails. But the true failure is the one who doesn't *learn* from his setbacks. That's why a teachable spirit is so important. When you are in the midst of a desert, the fastest way out of that desert is to ask God to let you learn everything that He has for you in that experience. Stay open, and stay teachable. God is not trying to ruin you. He is rebuilding you so that you can be used strategically. And the people God loves to use most are those who have learned to depend completely upon Him. For many of us self-sufficient, confident types, that doesn't come easily.

On a particular occasion, Winston Churchill got into an argument with one of his servants. "At the end of it, Churchill, his lower lip jutting, said: 'You were very rude to me, you know.' The servant, still seething, replied: 'Yes, but you were rude to me, too.' Churchill grumbled: 'Yes, but I am a great man.'"[6]

There was a visible flaw in the character of Churchill. His character was obviously not as refined or honed as Abraham Lincoln's. Lincoln was a man who had submitted his life to Jesus Christ. And the difference between the two "great" men could not have been drawn more clearly than in an incident that occurred late in the Civil War. Lincoln had just arrived in Richmond to view the city recently captured by Northern troops:

> Admiral Porter, with an escort of ten seamen, took the President up the river and into Richmond. He says that on landing they saw some twelve Negroes digging with spades. The leader of them was an old man sixty years of age. He raised himself to an upright position, put his hands up to his eyes, then dropped the spade and sprang forward.
>
> "Bress de Lord," he said, "dere is de great Messiah! I knowed him as soon as I seed him. He's been in my heart fo' long yeahs, an' he cum at las' to free his chillun from deir bondage! Glory, Hallelujah!"
>
> And he fell upon his knees before the President and kissed his feet. The others followed his example, and in a minute Mr. Lincoln was surrounded by these people, who had treasured up the recollection of him caught from a photograph, and had looked to him for four years as one who was to lead them out of captivity.
>
> Mr. Lincoln looked down at the poor creatures at his feet, and being embarrassed, said: "Don't kneel to me. That is not right. You must kneel to God only, and thank Him for the liberty you will hereafter enjoy. I am but God's humble instrument."[7]

Lincoln entertained large thoughts about God and small thoughts about himself. Humility means that someone has a proper self-confidence, a proper self-esteem, and a proper kind of godly courage. That kind of character only comes from being in the furnace of affliction and hardship. No wonder it was said that "the man Moses was very humble, more than any man who was on the face of the earth" (Numbers 12:3).

Do you feel like a failure? Then you are in good company. As John Gardner pointed out, "There are not many undefeated people around."

Our society is intoxicated with the idea of success. That's why we are so afraid of failure. But if you know Jesus Christ, you should know that failure, as Erwin Lutzer described it, can be the back door of success. The fact of the matter is this: God uses our failure to equip us for future success.

When you look behind the scenes at some of the most successful people in all of history, you will find that they were not unacquainted with failure. And it was failure that became the bedrock which enabled them to handle the triumphs that came later.

Have you become convinced that God has enrolled you in the M.C.A. program? Then you are in very, very good company, my friend. God doesn't enroll just anyone in this advanced course. He takes those for whom He has a special work and oversees every step of their higher education. And He is big enough and grand enough to take even our defeats and turn them to our ultimate advantage. For you see, some defeats are more triumphant than victories. But that's something only God can pull off.

When you graduate from this course, there will be no ceremony. No sheepskin diploma, no class ring, no cap and gown. But you will have the approval and certification of the Master Himself.

If that's not finishing strong, I don't know what is.

CHAPTER NINE

156 BUCK-NAKED
MILES TO BIGHORN

A man who wants to lead the orchestra
must turn his back on the crowd.

JAMES CROOK

O nly two men failed to return from the storied Lewis and Clark expedition
of the early 1800s.

One man failed to return because he got sick and died.

The other man failed to return because he was smitten.

He had just seen the length and breadth of what would one day become the
United States of America—from the Great Plains to the Rockies to the Columbia Basin of Oregon to the Pacific Ocean. His young eyes drank in what no
white man had ever seen, and the vast wonders of an unexplored continent had
a grip on his soul. So when Lewis and Clark set out for home, John Colter
waved them good-bye. He stayed on to explore the wide lands that were outside the scope of the expedition. He wanted to follow some of those trails and
paddle some of those rivers he'd passed by on the way to the Pacific. He was
haunted by their wild beauty.

Colter trapped beaver in the virgin streams of the high country. He was the
first white man to witness the geysers of Yellowstone. The young man's love

affair with uncharted lands kept him in constant danger. Close encounters with monster grizzlies, churning white-water rapids, and always dangerous Indians tested his courage, pluck, and reflexes. As years went by, he gained a legendary status among his fellow trappers and mountain men—men not easily impressed.

But the accomplishment that sealed Colter's reputation as a living legend wasn't a battle with a grizzly, shooting rapids in a fragile canoe, or scaling an unknown mountain range.

John Colter was best known for a single footrace.

It was a race that would be told and retold around campfires from the Columbia to the Missouri. John Colter had run like no man in history had ever run before.

It may have been because he was running for his life.

Colter had been trapping a particular stream with John Potts, an old friend from the Lewis and Clark expedition. As they were canoeing down a stretch of river not far from what today is Bozeman, Montana, they heard some rustling in the brush on both sides of the riverbank. In the next instant, they were surrounded by Blackfeet Indians with drawn bows.

There was no time for escape downstream. Colter did the only thing he could have done; he headed for the bank. As they were getting out of the canoe, a huge Indian ran forward and snatched Potts's rifle out of his hands. Colter, a man of great physical strength and courage, knew that any sign of fear would only ensure their tortuous death at the hands of these Blackfeet. The desperate trapper grabbed the rifle and wrestled it away from the Indian, throwing him to the ground in the process. He tossed the weapon back to Potts and turned to confront the startled warriors. Potts had seen enough and jumped into the canoe to make a getaway.

"NO!" shouted Colter, knowing there was no escape in that direction. Arrows rained into the canoe, killing Potts. The current swept the canoe and the body of Colter's friend downstream. Colter himself stood on the bank, unarmed and alone. The Blackfeet swarmed around him, stripped him naked, and then tied him down as they held a powwow, trying to determine what they should do with him.

"Skin him alive!"

"No, let's whip him to death!"

"Let's burn him alive!"

Then one of the Blackfeet came up with a creative idea. The chief approached Colter and asked him if he could run like a deer. Colter indicated that he was not as fast as the deer but slow as the turtle. This was a lie, for Colter was a remarkably fast runner. The chief, however, took the bait with a grin and quickly led everyone to a nearby sandy plain. He made a mark, and his warriors toed the line. He then took Colter and gave him a three-hundred-yard head start.

The buck-naked Colter took off like a shot. Except for moccasins and loin cloths, the pursuing Blackfeet were as naked as Colter. But each warrior carried his favorite weapon—and yearned for the honor of finishing off the white trapper.

The plain stretched ahead of Colter for six miles, dotted only by sagebrush and prickly pear. But shimmering on the horizon, Colter could see a line of trees on what must have been a bend of the river. He focused on those trees and began the run of his life.

Colter's bare feet were soon cut to bloody ribbons by the sharp stones and prickly pear, but in this race there was no stopping. One mile sped by. Two miles. At approximately three miles, Colter looked back over his shoulder, for he could no longer hear the yelling of his pursuers or the slap of their moccasins in the dust. Only a handful were still in the hunt, and they were a good distance away. One solitary brave, however, had closed to within two hundred yards. Colter's body was so stressed from the exertion of the chase that blood trickled from his mouth and nose.

At four miles Colter looked back again. The Indian, with protective moccasins on his feet, had gained a lot of ground, and was less than fifty yards away. Colter knew his broad, naked back was in range of the Indian's sharp lance. Without warning, the hunted man suddenly whirled and stopped, facing the

onrushing Indian and throwing his hands straight up in the air as if to surrender. The shocked Indian immediately threw his lance, and as it left his hand, he
stumbled and fell head over heels.

The lance fell short. Colter grabbed it and plunged it into his pursuer before
the exhausted Indian could regain his footing. Colter drove the lance into the
Indian with such force that the brave was pinned to the ground to die by his
own weapon.

Summoning every ounce of strength he had left, Colter ran the remaining
mile or so to the river and the stand of timber. Out in the middle of the stream
there was a sand bar, and at the head of this little island was a large raft of drift-
wood which had come down with the spring floods. Colter swam out to the
raft, dove beneath it, and came up where several of the entangled logs formed
a roof above his head. Here he waited for the pursuing Blackfeet, up to his neck
in the icy waters under his makeshift shelter.

He soon heard the approaching Blackfeet, who swarmed around the river,
onto the sand bar, and even stood upon the logs that covered Colter's head. But
they couldn't find him.

That terrible day, however, was still young, and the Blackfeet were wild to
avenge the death of their comrade. They kept up the hunt until late afternoon
before finally withdrawing. Under cover of darkness, John Colter swam downstream until he found a tiny stretch of bank concealed by trees and brush.
Naked, half-frozen, and nearly delirious from exposure and loss of blood, Colter
pulled himself out of the stream and lay gasping on the bank. He had no rifle,
no food, no fire, no horse, no shoes, and no clothing. He had been stripped of
everything. Everything but his will to live.

John Colter was half-dead and 150 miles away from the trading post at
Bighorn. Yet seven days later he walked naked, bleeding, and hungry into
the Bighorn compound. In that moment he became a living legend.[1]

Stripped of everything and against the worst odds imaginable, John Colter
outran and outsmarted the pursuing Blackfeet for 156 miles. In spite of everything, he managed to finish strong.

ANOTHER AMBUSH

In football, you suit up.

In running, you strip down.

That's why when you see the ESPN coverage of the Boston Marathon, those guys don't have helmets on their heads, pads on their shoulders, flak jackets on their torsos, braces on their knees, or high-top cleats on their feet.

If you were to throw those helmets, pads, jackets, braces, cleats, and several rolls of tape onto a scale, it would quickly be obvious that the average football player wears *pounds* of equipment.

Runners wear *ounces*.

Friend, the Christian life is not a contest that goes four quarters with occasional TV time-outs and Gatorade breaks on the sideline. In the Christian life, there is no midgame break called halftime. The Christian life is more like 26 miles and 385 yards.

No, that's not quite right.

The Christian life is more like 156 miles to Bighorn.

No time-outs. No halftime. No special teams. For a race like this you don't suit up. You strip down.

That's what happened to John Colter.

And that's what happened to Joseph.

Only he wasn't headed for Bighorn. He was going to Egypt.

Joseph's story begins at Genesis 37 and runs all the way to the end of the book in chapter 50. If you're not familiar with Joseph, it's a story that's well worth reading. If you like Tom Clancy or John Grisham, you'll love the biography of Joseph. It's a quick read, and nearly every paragraph adds another dimension to the plot. But for our purposes, allow me to give a thumbnail sketch of Joseph's life.

Joseph was the son of Jacob. Of Jacob's twelve sons, Joseph was the favorite. To show his love for Joseph, Jacob gave him this incredible multicolored coat he'd picked up on a business trip. Well, that really hacked off Joseph's brothers.

The other thing that hacked them off was that Joseph told them about a dream he'd had—a dream in which everyone in the family bowed low in his presence. Now these guys were all older than Joseph (except for his kid brother, Benjamin, who was home schooled and back at the house), and they had no intention of *ever* bowing down before Joseph.

One day Jacob sent Joseph to check on his brothers as they were overseeing their sheep flocks in a place called Shechem. That's when the tragedy occurred. Joseph ran into a war party of Blackfeet. Just kidding. Joseph didn't *need* Blackfeet. He had his brothers.

They saw Joseph coming from a distance and quickly decided that this was their chance to kill him. The oldest brother, Reuben, said it would be better if they didn't kill him. His plan was for them to throw Joseph into a pit and then he would come back and take Joseph home. But while Reuben was out of the picture, they decided to sell Joseph to a passing caravan and make some bucks off of him. Why kill him when they could pick up some extra cash and still get rid of him?

With Joseph on his way to slavery in Egypt, the brothers took his special coat and dipped it in animal blood. Then they went home and led Jacob to believe that Little Joe had been killed by a wild animal. That about did old Jacob in.

Meanwhile, Joseph was sold as a slave into the house of a guy named Potiphar, a high-ranking Egyptian official. It was only a matter of time before Joseph had so impressed Potiphar that the nobleman gave him oversight of the whole household. Faxes streamed in, phones rang off the hook, the FedEx and UPS guys were always at the door, and Joseph oversaw the whole operation. Potiphar completely trusted Joseph and apparently would only call his pager from time to time to check on how things were going.

Joseph was young and good looking. When his brothers sold him, he was an athletic seventeen years old. Somewhere along the line, Potiphar's wife started checking this young man out. Egyptian women of the ruling class were known for immorality, and this gal was no exception. She continually put the moves on Joseph, and though he was young and didn't even *know* all the moves, he continually held the woman off. But then one day when they were alone in the house, she cornered him. Joseph literally had to run right out of his tunic to get away. She accused him of attempted rape and Joseph wound up in the slammer.

But God was with Joseph, and it wasn't long before the young man was in charge of the prison! Through a miraculous series of events (well worth reading in all their amazing detail) Joseph emerged from prison as the Number Two man in all Egypt, answerable only to the Pharaoh himself.

Years went by, and famine ravaged that part of the world. Out of grain, Jacob sent his boys into Egypt to get what they needed from the new prime minister's well-managed granaries. To make a long story short, after juking his brothers around and messing with their minds for a while, the prime minister revealed himself to them as the long lost Joseph and directed them to go home and bring the entire family to Egypt. And it was one heck of a reunion as they all bowed before Joseph, the son Jacob thought he would never see again.

John Locke's wise observation is worth noting:

> The great question which, in all ages, has disturbed mankind and
> brought on them the greatest part of those mischiefs which have
> ruined cities, depopulated countries, and disordered the peace of the
> world, has been, not whether there be power in the world…but who
> should have it.[2]

God decided that Joseph should have that power. And He gave it to him in a moment. The young man hit a huge career updraft that lifted him from prison to palace in a little over two years.

So you think that you're trapped in your circumstances? Think again, pal. I don't know what your situation might be, but I can guess that Joseph could out-circumstance circles around you. Your family may not appreciate you as much as you'd like, but they've probably stopped short of selling you into slavery. You may have it tough, but you're probably not cooling your heels in a foreign dungeon on a rape charge. And remember, there was no parole board

FINISHING STRONG

to review Joseph's case. Unlike our court system, when those Egyptian boys said life, they meant L-I-F-E.

Those were the hopeless circumstances of Joseph's life. Until God stepped in and whispered a word in Pharaoh's ear. "NOW," He said. "Now is the time. He's My man, and he's ready. Promote him." And Pharaoh immediately obeyed the God he didn't know and didn't serve and promoted Joseph.

Are you worried that you don't have much of a network? Joseph didn't either. But he had a Friend in High Places. And if you have surrendered your life to Christ, so do you. It's all the network you'll ever need.

The story of Joseph is nothing less than amazing. The principles that are found in the life of Joseph could easily fill an entire book. But we're almost at the end of *this* book, so we're going to have go directly to the bottom line.

You remember John Colter? He was stripped of everything, but in spite of that, he still finished strong. I've got a question for you. Was Colter really stripped of everything?

The answer is no.

- Colter was stripped of his clothes but not of his courage.
- Colter was stripped of his weapons but not of his will.
- Colter was stripped of his provisions but not of his purpose.
- Colter was stripped of his comforts but not of his composure.

That's why he reminds me of Joseph.

- Joseph was stripped of his coat but not of his character.
- Joseph was stripped of his family but not of his future.
- Joseph was stripped of his position but not of his purity.
- Joseph was stripped of his accomplishments but not of his attitude.

No wonder Joseph finished strong.

John Colter really does remind me of Joseph. But the more I look at Joseph, the more he reminds me of Jesus. Joseph and Jesus had a lot in common.

- Joseph was rejected by his brothers. So was Jesus.
- Joseph was loved by his father. So was Jesus.
- Joseph was victorious over temptation. So was Jesus.

- Joseph was taken into custody because of a false witness. So was Jesus.
- Joseph suffered for doing what was right. So did Jesus.
- Joseph was promoted from prison to rule the nation. Jesus was promoted from the prison of death to rule the nations.

And there's one more thing that Joseph had in common with Jesus. Like Jesus, Joseph finished strong.

> Therefore, since we have so great a cloud of witnesses surrounding us, let us also lay aside every encumbrance, and the sin which so easily entangles us, and let us run with endurance the race that is set before us, fixing our eyes on Jesus, the author and perfector of faith, who for the joy set before Him endured the cross, despising the shame, and has sat down at the right hand of the throne of God. (Hebrews 12:1–2)

Jesus finished strong.

Some guy may be thinking, "Of course He finished strong. He's *God.*"

That's true. He is God and you would expect God to finish strong. But you don't have to be God to finish strong. You just have to *depend* on God. That's actually what Jesus did when He was on earth. And once again, Joseph and Jesus have something in common. For that's precisely what Joseph did, too. His dependence was completely upon the God of his fathers.

Let me ask you a question. Whom are you depending on? Yourself? Forget it. Some political leader? Give me a break. As James Boren said, "It's hard to look up to a leader who keeps his ear to the ground."

Joseph didn't have his ear to the ground. His ear was tuned to another station.

> Things which eye has not seen and ear has not heard, and which have not entered the heart of man, all that God has prepared for those who love him. (1 Corinthians 2:9)

Joseph loved God with his whole heart. And that's why, wherever he found himself—whether in Potiphar's house or prison or the palace—he was quickly promoted to run the whole shootin' match. Egypt may have been full of leaders, but none of them was like Joseph. Here was a young man who walked with God.

ON YOUR MARK... GET SET...

Seventeen-year-old Joseph didn't know it, but when he left his father's house to go find his brothers and the sheep, he was about to commence the race of his life. And as we have seen, when you're in a race like that, you don't suit up. You strip down.

To be more specific, there are two parts to the stripping-down process.

- *There are the things that God strips from us.*
- *There are the things that we strip from ourselves.*

Or to put it another way:

- *There are things that God will take away.*
- *There are things which we must put away.*

Joseph finished strong. I want to finish strong. You want to finish strong. So then, we must do exactly what Joseph did and "also lay aside every encumbrance, and the sin which so easily entangles us, and let us run with endurance the race that is set before us, fixing our eyes on Jesus."

If we are going to finish strong, there are some things that we are going to have to put away. And I see two very critical things Joseph put away that enabled him to finish his race with a strong kick.

- *Joseph put away the thought of trading his purity for his position.*
- *Joseph put away the thought of turning his betrayal into bitterness.*

HE PUT AWAY THE THOUGHT OF TRADING HIS PURITY FOR HIS POSITION

Joseph was no fool. He knew that ultimately there would be a price to pay for resisting the sexual favors of Potiphar's wife. No matter how many times you may have read this little account, please take a minute or two to review this most critical test in one young man's life.

> And it came about after these events that his master's wife looked with desire at Joseph, and she said, "Lie with me." But he refused and said to his master's wife, "Behold, with me here, my master does not concern himself with anything in the house, and he has put all that he owns in my charge. There is no one greater in this house than I, and he has withheld nothing from me except you, because you are his wife. How then could I do this great evil, and sin against God?" And it came about as she spoke to Joseph day after day, that he did not listen to her to lie beside her, or be with her. Now it happened one day that he went into the house to do his work, and none of the men of the household was there inside. And she caught him by his garment, saying, "Lie with me!" And he left his garment in her hand and fled, and went outside. When she saw that he had left his garment in her hand, and had fled outside, she called to the men of her household, and said to them, "See, he has brought in a Hebrew to us to make sport of us; he came in to me to lie with me, and I screamed. And it came about when he heard that I raised my voice and screamed, that he left his garment beside me and fled, and went outside." So she left his garment beside her until his master came home. Then she spoke to him with these words, "The Hebrew slave, whom you brought to us, came in to me to make sport of me; and it happened as I raised my voice and screamed, that he left his garment beside me and fled outside."
>
> Now it came about when his master heard the words of his wife, which she spoke to him, saying, "This is what your slave did to me," that his anger burned. So Joseph's master took him and put him into the jail, the place where the king's prisoners were confined; and he was there in jail. (Genesis 39:7–20)

Joseph was a unique man. And that's why he was so greatly used. He had been tested. And he passed those tests with flying colors because of his willingness to put some things away.

Did you catch his response to the invitation of Potiphar's wife? Joseph said, "How then could I do this great evil, and sin against God?" There's your difference between finishing strong and finishing so-so. Joseph was not willing to participate with her sexually because it was a *great evil*. Yet to her it was great fun.

The man who finishes so-so has kept back one or two areas of his life from the Lord. His theme song is *"I Surrender Ninety-five Percent."* In his heart he knows what he is doing is a great evil, but he's not willing to give up his great fun.

The man who finishes strong keeps back nothing from the Lord. He is brutal in dealing with sin in his own life because he does not want to dishonor God's name and holiness. So when it comes to sin, or "great evil," as Joseph called it, he doesn't coddle it, he doesn't favor it, and he doesn't hold on to it. He gets rid of it. His theme song is *"I Surrender All."* That's it. That's the secret.

I surrender *all*.

Not most.

All.

That's what separates the men from the boys in this 156-mile race to Bighorn.

Or Egypt.

Or heaven.

By the way, what was this woman's name? The text doesn't tell us and it gets a little tiresome referring to her as "Potiphar's wife" or "Mrs. Potiphar." So to make things easy, I'm going to give her a name. How about Potiphar and... *Predator*. Sort of has a nice ring to it, doesn't it? You can almost see it engraved in wood in the window of their Winnebago. For that's exactly what this woman was. She was a predator. And she was stalking Joseph from the first day she laid eyes on him.

Do you think that Satan had a clue of what God had in mind for Joseph? I don't for a minute think that he knew the whole picture, but as Louis L'Amour would say, he was always good at reading sign. I think the enemy pieced together enough clues to realize that Joseph was a man God intended to use. So he hit Joseph with an all-out, frontal assault.

Normally, it's the man who pursues the woman. But not always. And the enemy sent one of his first stringers to go one-on-one with the young Israelite. And if I were a betting man, I'd put cash on the table that she was a hooker...I mean a looker. Come to think of it, she was probably both.

The story is told of the famous author who was attending a lavish dinner party held in his honor. He was seated next to a very sophisticated and stylish young woman. She was stunningly beautiful and elegant. At one point during the meal, he leaned over and discreetly whispered in her ear, "Would you be willing to sleep with me tonight for twenty-five thousand dollars?"

The woman smiled coyly and silently nodded a yes.

He leaned once again and whispered to her, "How about fifty bucks?"

The woman was horrified. She lost her composure and yelled at the author, "Just what do you think I am?"

The author replied, "We have already established that. We are simply discussing the price."

Joseph knew what Predator was and that her price to him was free. At least...there was no price on the surface. But Joseph was wise enough to know two things. She was not what he wanted, and she was not worth what she would cost. What would she cost Joseph? She would cost him everything. And he was smart enough to know it. It's tragic how many Christian men don't stop to count the cost *before* the opportunity presents itself. For sin will *always* cost you more than you wanted to pay.

Joseph probably had to count that cost just about every day. She was always there, always inviting, always displaying her wares, instantly available. But Joseph steeled himself on a daily basis. And it cost him. Sin will always cost you, but sometimes purity can cost you, too. But that's a price that strong finishers are always willing to pay.

So how much was Joseph willing to pay to keep his purity? Joseph was willing to strip himself of a coveted position (and one that he could never hope to attain again) in order to keep his integrity.

I met a guy just last week who did the same thing. As we were talking over lunch, he told me of his refusal to trade his purity for his position. (Can you believe it? Three thousand years later and the enemy is still trying to pick off God's men using the lure of sexual temptation. It's one of the oldest tools in his tool chest, and it just keeps working.) My friend gave me permission to let you in on his struggle with the enemy on this very issue.

Let's call this guy Frank. Frank is a very solid guy in his midthirties who is committed to Christ and to his wife and children. But he found himself being drawn emotionally to a woman he worked with. Interestingly enough, she was also a Christian. And they were friends.

Nothing ever happened between Frank and this woman. He never touched her or expressed anything inappropriate to her. And she certainly wasn't making any moves toward him. But due to the daily closeness of their working conditions, Frank began to realize he was being drawn to this woman. And he realized that his emotions were beginning to come into play. He would find himself thinking about her at odd times. He looked forward to being with her.

And then it began to dawn on him what was really happening. He had read my book *Point Man* several months earlier. And in *Point Man*, he read that before a man ever falls sexually, he first falls emotionally.

Frank realized that was happening to him. It was so subtle, so innocent. But the Holy Spirit was sending a wire to Frank that he was heading for an iceberg. So what did he do?

The first thing he did was to tell his wife.

I'm not kidding.

He told her that absolutely nothing had happened and *wouldn't* happen. He loved her and the kids more than she could know. But he wanted her to know that he was dealing with an emotional attraction to this Christian woman who was a friend to both of them.

Now notice that this guy didn't ignore the wire. He didn't keep steaming on straight ahead like an arrogant *Titanic*. He didn't assume he was "unsinkable." In fact, he shared the situation with his wife because he wanted her to know what was going on in his heart. And then together they prayed that the Lord would help him to overcome this attraction that he was facing at work every day. Several weeks went by, however, and he was still struggling. The undertow was still strong. Things weren't getting better. After consulting again with his wife, he decided to take the next appropriate step. He decided to look for another job.

Now Frank had an excellent position. But he found himself losing focus on his job and his family because of the emotional attraction that he was fighting off every day. So he decided that the best thing to do was to get another job. You could say that he wasn't willing to trade his purity for his position. Or you could say that he was "fleeing immorality." Joseph fled and left his garment. Frank fled and left his job. *But they both kept their purity.*

But nothing had happened! That's right. Nothing had happened…yet. And this guy was smart enough to take some measures to ensure that nothing *would* happen. So he did something about it and changed his professional address. He had received several inquiries from other companies, and within just a couple of weeks he was working for another employer. No, this was no promotion; it was nothing more than a lateral move. But I'll guarantee you this. He got a promotion at home. His wife thinks the world of him because he was not willing to risk the sanctity of their relationship by staying in a situation that was becoming too hot for him to handle.

Guys change jobs all the time.

Some will change for a promotion.

Some will change for power.

Few have the guts to change for purity. But those are the guys who make it all the way to Bighorn.

HE PUT AWAY THE THOUGHT OF TURNING HIS BETRAYAL INTO BITTERNESS

As I reflect on the life of Joseph, I can't help but think about what must have been a gnawing temptation for him: to become bitter at those who had betrayed him.

I really like the way Chuck Swindoll has put it:

> No one who does a serious study of Joseph's life would deny that he was a great man. And yet he never accomplished any of the things we normally associate with biblical greatness. He never slew a giant. He never wrote a line of Scripture or made any vast prophetic predictions like Daniel. Come to think of it, Joseph never even performed a single miracle. He was just your typical boy next door, who grew up in a very troubled family.
>
> So what made Joseph great? Why does God devote more space in Genesis to his story than to any other individual's? *Because of Joseph's attitude, how he responded to difficult circumstances.* That was the most remarkable thing about him.
>
> American author Elbert Hubbard once wrote, "The final proof of greatness lies in being able to endure (contemptuous treatment) *without resentment.*" Joseph spent a good deal of his life enduring harsh, hateful treatment, and his attitude during those years offers indisputable proof of his greatness. [3]

If anyone ever had the right to become bitter, it was Joseph. Think about it. He was sold into slavery by his brothers at the age of seventeen. And the only reason that they sold him instead of killing him outright was to pick up some beer money. That's what you call betrayal.

Then he gets to Egypt and is faithful to God and to Potiphar by resisting Predator. Yet he winds up in another pit, even deeper and darker than the first. That's also what you call betrayal. And he did nothing to deserve it. In fact, he did what was right.

From a distorted human perspective, Joseph had grounds for bitterness against:

- his brothers
- Potiphar
- Predator
- God

As Joseph sat in his cell playing solitaire, he had plenty of time to stew in the juices of bitterness. But he didn't. Joseph was smart enough to know that bitterness, like a burning match, only burns the one who holds onto it. Years later, when his brothers came to him seeking grain, he had his opportunity for revenge. Joseph lawfully had the power of life and death over them. Joseph now had the power that few men ever possess. As Abraham Lincoln said, "Nearly all men can stand adversity, but if you want to test a man's character, give him power."

That power could *easily* have been used to destroy his brothers and Predator, those chief instigators of pain and suffering in his life. Years apart, they both betrayed him. But he didn't go after them. He didn't destroy them. He blessed them.

Few men have withstood the adversity that Joseph went through as a result of being betrayed. But far fewer have refused to take revenge upon their enemies once they were in a position of power to do so. As Elbert Hubbard noted with amazement, Joseph lived *"without resentment."*

But do I hear you saying that you have good reason to be bitter?

- You were betrayed by your wife.
- You were betrayed by your best friend.
- You were betrayed by your Christian business partner.
- You were betrayed by the guy who led you to Christ.

Listen, I know that you've been deeply wronged. Perhaps like Joseph, your life has been brought to utter ruin. But you've got your focus in the wrong place. If you are focusing on some person or what he did to you, you *will not* finish strong. You'll never make it. You are being conned and you are being set up. You can only finish strong if you fix your eyes on Jesus.

When we are betrayed and tempted to become bitter, the real issue is *perspective*. The temptation is to think that some person has ruined you, has irreparably damaged your life and reputation in a way that can never be fixed. That simply isn't true.

God is in charge of your life—and over all the events and circumstances that touch you in any way. And this betrayal that you have suffered was allowed by Him to enter your life.

God is able to take the hateful and hurtful motivations of your enemies and use them to accomplish His plan in your life. These things won't keep you from God's best...they will help you to reach God's best. For it is in the deep and dark experiences of betrayal, when we wrestle with the giant of bitterness, that we begin to build spiritual muscle. As you grapple with the hurt and humiliation and fight off the desire to become a hardened, bitter person, you are actually building the spiritual muscle tone that it takes to finish strong.

But don't get your eyes off Jesus. Keep focused on Him just like John Colter focused on those trees in the distance.

Go to Him. *Run* to Him. He understands your betrayal because He Himself was betrayed. He knows what it feels like. So pour it all out to Him. Tell Him everything you're feeling. Flush out your system to Him. He knows it all anyway. Get it all out. Every ounce of hurt. Every old video clip in your memory.

And then forget it.

It's time to grow up.

It's time to move on.

It's time to quit being a victim.

Good night, if anyone had a right to wear the label "victim" for the rest of his life, it was Joseph. But he didn't wallow in self-pity, and he didn't soak in a hot tub of bitterness. Joseph's God was bigger than that. His brothers intended it for evil, but God intended it for good. Joseph never would have realized the good that God had in store for him if he had held on to the bitterness. And neither will you.

Who are the "brothers" in your life? Who is the Predator on your case? Yes, these people may intend evil for you. But God intends good. You will see that more and more as the days go by—but you have to get rid of that bitterness before He can work.

> And do not grieve the Holy Spirit of God, by whom you were sealed for the day of redemption. Let all *bitterness* and wrath and anger and clamor and slander be put away from you, along with all malice. And be kind to one another, tender-hearted, forgiving each other, just as God in Christ also has forgiven you. (Ephesians 4:30–32)

Your bitterness is grieving the Spirit of God.

Your bitterness is poisoning your soul.

Your bitterness is slowing your race and letting the enemy gain ground on you.

I'm reminded of a young man who was having a significant ministry in a small English village many years ago. People were coming from miles around to hear him teach the Scriptures. In his midtwenties, he had a voracious appetite for not only teaching the Scriptures but knowing them as well. He was making an impact in the village and the surrounding area. Until the charges were made.

A young woman came forward and claimed that he had tried to force himself upon her sexually. The word spread like wildfire across the countryside. He was finished. The sentiments of the people were with the young girl. His reputation was in shambles. *And it was all a lie.* It simply never happened.

The young man struggled deeply with the betrayal of the young woman whom he had legitimately tried to help. But she had turned on him and was in the process of ruining his ministry for life. He thought he would never recover. How could he ever minister again anywhere with such charges against him?

Bitterness just about overwhelmed him. The betrayal was too much. He couldn't bear it and he couldn't undo it. But with God's help, he refused to allow that bitterness to take root in his heart. God enabled him to conquer the bitterness just as Joseph had conquered it. The falsely accused young man thought that he would never again be used by God. But there are millions of people who can vouch for the fact that Oswald Chambers was greatly used of God before it was all over. To this day his book, *My Utmost for His Highest*, tops the Christian bestseller list.

Oswald Chambers struggled with betrayal and bitterness and finished strong.

Joseph struggled with betrayal and bitterness but he finished strong.

Perhaps you are struggling with betrayal and bitterness. You're certainly in good company, aren't you? For you have the same God that they trusted in. And if you will let Him, He will give you the same perspective that He gave to both of them. And you too, will finish strong.

You've got 156 miles ahead of you, my friend.

So do what John Colter did. Take the lance of the Word of God and drive it through the very heart of that pursuing bitterness. Pin that thing to the ground. And get on with the race. The sooner you get on with it, the sooner you will discover the blessings that God has for you. Trust me. They are beyond anything you could ever ask, dream, or imagine. And when you finally run into them, they'll take your breath away.

Just ask Joseph.

CHAPTER TEN

A VISION FOR THE FINISH LINE

———⊃

*Only he who can see the invisible
can do the impossible.*

FRANK GAINES

I t was the first time away from home for Walt.

It was the first time away from home for Ray.

They were in the army now.

Their bunks were just a few feet from each other. They got up early together, marched together, and did K.P. together.

Even in those days, they both had it.

But Walt didn't know that Ray had it, and Ray didn't know that Walt had it.

What they both had was vision.

They were only in those barracks together for a few months, and then they got separate orders, and their brief friendship came to an end.

But they never lost their vision.

Walt, who was always drawing in his spare time, didn't take long to make his mark. He was a fast starter. But Walt had too much vision to be just an artist. He had enough vision to turn those doodles into Mickey Mouse, and enough vision to turn Mickey into a studio, and enough vision to turn the Walt Disney

Studios into Disneyland, and enough vision before he died to lay out the plans for Epcot and Disney World in Florida. No doubt about it. Walt had vision.

So did Ray. But Ray didn't come out of the blocks as fast as Walt did. Now don't get me wrong. Ray was doing just fine in business. No doubt about it. Ray could sell. He was the highest paid salesman in his company. But Ray really didn't come into his own until he pulled into the hamburger stand in San Bernardino that was owned by the McDonald brothers. Ray sold Multimixer milk shake machines around the country to diners and small restaurants. Most of those mom and pop operations had one Multimixer with five spindles that could make five shakes. The McDonald brothers had *eight* Multimixers going full blast from start to close. Plus, they had developed a system that turned out fifteen-cent burgers and French fries like Chevies coming off a Detroit assembly line.

Ray had the vision to see what the McDonald brothers couldn't. He was fifty-two years old, and he had diabetes and arthritis. But he still had vision. And Ray Kroc drove out of San Bernardino with a contract that gave him the right to do what the McDonalds didn't think they could do and didn't want to try. And the rest is history.

Two young guys sitting on their bunks in a dusty old army barracks. No one would have guessed that those two young soldiers would be two of the greatest visionaries in the history of America.

So what's the big deal about vision? Some people have it, some don't. The big deal about vision is this.

It takes vision to finish strong.

Let me ask you a question. What do you want your life to look like in ten years? How about twenty years? Let me ask you another question. What do you want your children's lives to look like in ten years? To put it bluntly, the quality of life that your kids enjoy ten years from now will, to a great degree, depend upon the choices *you* will make in that ten-year period of time. And the same goes for twenty years.

David Blankenhorn, in his insightful book *Fatherless America*, proves the point:

> The United States is becoming an increasingly fatherless society. A
> generation ago, an American child could reasonably expect to grow up
> with his or her father. Today, an American child can reasonably expect
> not to. Fatherlessness is now approaching a rough parity with
> fatherhood as a defining feature of American childhood.
>
> This astonishing fact is reflected in many statistics, but here are
> the two most important. Tonight, about 40 percent of American
> children will go to sleep in homes in which their fathers do not live.
> Before they reach the age of eighteen, more than *half* of our nation's
> children are likely to spend at least a significant portion of their
> childhood living apart from their fathers. Never before in this country
> have so many children been voluntarily abandoned by their fathers.
> Never before have so many children grown up without knowing what
> it means to have a father. [1]

What is your vision for your life? We can no longer afford to define that vision just in terms of building a successful career or a business. Building Epcots and Golden Arches pales into insignificance when compared to the challenge of building a family. A *godly* family. Yes, we are to provide for our families. But there is something that is so wonderful and so marvelous and so rare and so exceptional, that if we succeed in giving this one thing to our families, then we will have succeeded like few men ever succeed. What is this wonderful provision that so few men offer their children?

It is the example of a strong finish.

Listen to Blankenhorn's insight one more time:

> Fatherlessness is the most harmful demographic trend of this
> generation.... If this trend continues, fatherlessness is likely to change

the shape of our society. Consider this prediction. After the year 2000, as people born after 1970 emerge as a large proportion of our working-age adult population, the United States will be a nation divided into two groups, separate and equal. The two groups will work in the same economy, speak a common language, and remember the same national history. But they will live fundamentally divergent lives. One group will receive basic benefits—psychological, social, economic, educational and moral—that are denied to the other group.

The primary fault line dividing the two groups will not be race, religion, class, education, or gender. It will be patrimony. One group will consist of those adults who grew up with daily presence and provision of fathers. The other group will consist of those who did not.[2]

I've been making an assumption about you. I've been assuming that you are a Christian. I've been assuming that you are serious about following Christ. If you weren't serious about your faith, you wouldn't have gotten this far.

I'm also assuming that you are married and have at least a couple of kids. And I'm assuming that most of you singles will one day be married with a couple of kids.

And, of course, I'm assuming that you love your wife. And you love your kids.

And because of all these assumptions, I'm also assuming something else. You've got an enemy who hates your guts and will do anything to keep you from finishing strong.

Blankenhorn is right. We have a crisis of fatherhood. Our kids will grow up to be a part of one of those two groups. They will either be in the haves or the have nots. What is so tragic is that many Christian fathers who leave their families do so because they have no vision.

Your kids deserve better than that. Your Lord deserves better than that. You *must* be a man of vision. Not just for this month or for next year but for forty or fifty years out.

It's time to wise up, gentlemen.

We're not going to finish strong by luck.

We're not going to finish strong by taking life as it comes.

In order to finish strong, we must have vision. Vision for what is really important, vision for what our kids really need, and the vision to steel ourselves against the strategies of the enemy to destroy everything near and dear to our hearts.

It's that kind of vision that helps us to make choices with our heads and not our sex organs. It's that kind of vision that will enable us to leave a legacy to our children that most of the kids in America can only dream about.

This book has been about vision. The vision to finish strong.

What does it mean to finish strong? It means that you will come to the end of your life with a strong and close relationship to Christ. It means that, unless God has taken your wife ahead of you, you will be married to the same woman that you are today. It means that you are a man who is in the Scriptures and living the Scriptures. It means that you are a man who has fought some battles for the kingdom and has the scars to prove it. To finish strong means that you are leaving your children and grandchildren the *priceless* heritage of a godly life.

To do that takes vision. Especially if you're in your twenties or thirties. Few men have the vision at that age to look forty years into the future and think about how they want to finish.

It takes vision to do it when you're in your forties and fifties. For that's when so many guys get sloppy spiritually and put it all on cruise control. Oh, they'll finish, all right. But they won't finish strong.

It takes vision in your sixties and seventies to realize that those little grandchildren are the leaders of a future generation. And it takes vision to spend time with them instead of cruising the country six months out of the year in a Winnebago.

Maybe you didn't realize it, but this whole book has been about vision.

It takes vision to see that the majority of men who start strong don't finish strong. So it takes vision *early* to be the one guy out of ten who does.

It takes vision to anticipate and avoid the ambushes.

It takes vision to stay in, to stay close, to stay away, and to stay alert.

It takes vision to avoid dry shipwrecks.

It takes vision to pray that God will alert you every day to the killing dangers of pride.

It takes vision to see the benefit of making yourself accountable and teachable.

It takes vision to be willing to go through the miserable, gut-wrenching dry heaves of genuine repentance that will put you back on course.

It takes vision to hang in there and finish your master's degree in Character Acquisition. Especially when you don't have a clue when you will graduate.

It takes vision to run 156 miles to Bighorn and not trade in your purity in the process.

It takes vision not to finish poorly.

It takes vision not to finish so-so.

It takes vision to finish strong.

Your wife will love for it.

Your kids, twenty and thirty years down the line, when *they* are raising kids, will thank God for a dad who didn't flake out when things got tough. And they won't flake out either. Because they saw the key man in their life finish strong.

You may not feel at this point in your life that you are really making a mark. You may feel that you're just sort of average and not really making a difference. My friend Dave Roper has felt like that. Hear his wise words as we wrap up this little journey together:

> So you're not a major player. So you have no political clout or power base. So you're not a Christian quarterback, a converted rock star, a multi-media personality, or a multi-millionaire.
>
> You can be a catalyst for change.
>
> You can be used to arrest the spread of corruption in your community.
>
> You can be a source of light in your dark corner of society.

You can be the means by which some part of our crazy world is brought into sync.

We are all designed to be of incalculable use to God. He planned our usefulness before time began. "We are God's workmanship," Paul insists, "created in Christ Jesus to do good works, which God prepared in advance for us to do" (Ephesians 2:10).

Perhaps it will be a visible role, more likely it's concealed and hidden. It could be that your entire life will find its meaning in one person whom God wants you to touch in some significant way—in one event in which he yearns to make himself known.

I do not know what God will do with you and me, but I know this: When we stand before our Lord one day, our lives will not be without meaning. "No one is without a divinely appointed task," John Ruskin said, "and the divine means for getting it done."

"But," you ask, "how will I know when my moment has come? How can I integrate and focus my life on that one duty that God has for me today? The world has a thousand necessities. Issues clamor every day for my attention. What will keep me from being manipulated by every cause and craze?"[3]

Vision will enable you to keep your daily focus.
Vision will enable you to be faithful each day.
Vision will enable you to fix your eyes on Jesus.

If you could go back in a time machine, two thousand years ago, to the times of the New Testament, it might give you some perspective.

If you were to plant yourself in a busy market near the temple in Jerusalem, you could gather some real insight. Stop and think what it would be like to randomly interview the citizens of Jerusalem as they went about their daily business in the times of the early church.[4]

You would only need to ask them a couple of questions.

"Who do you think that people two thousand years from now will remember from your generation?"

My guess is, many of those citizens of the Roman Empire would answer, "Caesar." Others would respond, "Nero."

"But what about this group of people known as Christians. Don't you think that anyone will remember them or their leaders?"

"Are you kidding? That group of nobodies? They don't have any influence. They aren't important."

"You mean you haven't heard of Paul or Peter? Don't you think they'll be remembered? Or what about Mary and Martha? Wasn't their brother involved in some miracle?"

"I'm telling you, these people are insignificant. The only thing I ever hear of their leaders is that they're always winding up in jail. Trust me, in two thousand years, nobody will give them a thought."

So here we are, two thousand years later. And isn't it interesting that we name our children Peter and Paul, Mary and Martha?

And we name our dogs Caesar and Nero.

You are doing something very significant, my friend.

And He sees it.

No wonder you're going to finish strong.

NOTES

Chapter One: One Out of Ten

1. William Martin, *A Prophet with Honor: The Billy Graham Story* (New York: William Morrow, 1991), 112.

2. Ibid., 110.

3. Ibid.

4. John Haggai, *Lead On!* (Dallas: Word, 1986), 72.

5. John MacArthur, *How to Meet the Enemy* (Wheaton, Ill.: Victor Books, 1992), 67.

6. Ruth Tucker, *Stories of Faith* (Grand Rapids: Zondervan, 1989).

7. Billy Graham, *A Biblical Standard for Evangelists* (Minneapolis: World Wide Publications, 1984), 74.

Chapter Two: Finishing So-So

1. U. S. Department of the Interior, U. S. Geological Survey, *John Wesley Powell: Soldier, Explorer, Scientist* (1969), 1.

2. J. Robert Clinton, *The Mantle of the Mentor* (Altadena, Calif.: Barnabas Publishing, 1993), 4.

3. Ibid., 5.

4. Ibid.

5. Ibid.

6. Ibid.

7. Howard Hendricks, phone interview by author, May, 1995.

8. Martin, *A Prophet with Honor,* 566.

9. Stu Weber, *Along the Road to Manhood* (Sisters, Ore: Multnomah, 1995), 55.

Chapter Three: Staying the Course

1. Bob Buford, *Halftime* (Grand Rapids, Mich.: Harper Collins-Zondervan, 1994), 77.

2. Ibid., 67.

3. Stephen R. Covey, *The Seven Habits of Highly Effective People* (New York: Simon and Schuster, 1989), 106.

4. Cited by Rod Handley, *Character Counts—Who's Counting Yours?* (Grand Island, Neb.: Cross Trainer Publishing, 1995), 18.

5. "The Sex Life of America's Christians," *Leadership,* Summer 1995, 31.

6. Ibid.

7. Ibid.

8. "Traits of a Sexually Healthy Pastor," *Leadership,* Summer 1995, 21.

9. David Roper, *Seeing Through* (Sisters, Ore.: Questar, 1995), 22.

10. D. Martyn Lloyd-Jones, *The Christian Warfare* (Grand Rapids, Mich.: Baker, 1976), 41.

Chapter Four: Dry Shipwreck

1. Max Lucado, *The Inspirational Study Bible* (Dallas: Word, 1995), 323.

2. Mark Twain, *Life on the Mississippi.*

3. John P. Eaton and Charles A. Haas, *Titanic: Destination Disaster* (New York: Norton and Co., 1987), 19.

4. F. B. Meyer, *Great Men of the Bible,* vol. 2 (Grand Rapids, Mich.: Zondervan, 1982), 58.

5. Eaton and Haas, *Titanic,* 7.

6. Meyer, *Great Men,* 59.

7. Lucado, *The Inspirational Study Bible,* 323.

Chapter Five: The Status Brothers and Their Not-Quite-Right First Cousin, Pride

1. Anthony Campolo, cited by John Johnston, *Christian Excellence* (Grand Rapids: Baker, 1985).

Chapter Six: UnTeachable, UnAccountable, and UnAcceptable

1. *Wolf Street Foundation Newsletter,* Little Rock, Arkansas.

Chapter Eight: Failure That Equips You to Finish

1. Meyer, *Great Men,* 157.

2. Ibid, 686.

3. Ibid, 687.

4. Cited by Dean Ornish, *Program for Reversing Heart Disease* (New York: Random House, 1990), 91.

5. Miles Sanford, *The Green Letters* (n.p.)

6. William Manchester, *The Last Lion: Winston Spencer Churchill* (New York: Little, Brown, 1985), 36.

7. G. Frederick Owen, *Abraham Lincoln: The Man and His Faith* (Wheaton, Ill.: Tyndale, 1981), 195.

Chapter Nine: 156 Buck-Naked Miles to Bighorn

1. I have used two primary sources for the story of John Colter: Charles Johnston, *Famous Frontiersmen* (Boston: Colonial Press, 1913), 122–28, and Frederick R. Bechdolt, *Giants of the Old West* (Freeport, N.Y.: Meredith Press, 1930), 14–21. Another excellent source is Burton Harris, *John Colter: His Years in the Rockies* (New York: Charles Scribner's Sons, 1952).

2. The Forbes Leadership Library, *Thoughts on Leadership* (Chicago: Triumph Books, 1995).

3. Charles R. Swindoll, *Joseph: From Pit to Pinnacle* (Anaheim, Calif.: Insight for Living Publishing, 1990), 75.

Chapter Ten: A Vision for the Finish Line

1. David Blankenhorn, *Fatherless America* (New York: Basic Books, 1995), 1.

2. Ibid.

3. Roper, *Seeing Through,* 22, 26.

4. This scenario is not original to me. I first heard it years ago at a Family Life Marriage Conference.

STUDY GUIDE

ONE OUT OF TEN

1. Steve writes, "In the Christian life, it's not how you start that matters. It's how you finish."

   A. How did you start in the Christian life? Describe how you came to know the Savior.

   B. Pick a single word to describe your Christian experience to this point (examples: steady, uneven, growing, disappointing, rocky, exciting, etc.). Why did you pick this word? Are you satisfied with this description? Why or why not?

   C. In a paragraph or two, describe how you would like to be remembered on the day of your funeral. Do you think you're on track to be remembered in this way? Why or why not? What would you have to change *today* to make it more likely that such a scenario could actually take place?

2. What does it mean to you to "finish strong"? Describe someone you know personally who finished strong in life. What did he do to cause you to think this way about him?

3. Steve writes that most men are "shot down" by one of the following enemies:
   moral failure
   discouragement
   liberal theology
   money
   alcohol
   apostasy

   A. Which of these enemies are most likely to give you the most trouble? Why?

   B. What are you doing to combat each one of these enemies? How could you become even more effective against them?

4. Steve writes, "Men who don't hit the finish line strong have *chosen* to remove themselves from the Lord's protection and power."

   A. How does a man "choose" to remove himself from God's protection and power? Describe any examples of this that you can recall.

B. Do you think such a choice is more likely a process or a one-time decision? Explain your answer.

C. Are you firmly within the Lord's protection and power? Explain your answer.

5. Read Hebrews 12:1–3.

A. What are we instructed to do in verse 1? Why is the word "perseverance" (NIV) so crucial here?

B. What are we instructed to do in verse 2? What example is given to us? How is this example supposed to help us?

C. What are we instructed to do in verse 3? What reason is given for this instruction?

6. Read Acts 20:24.

A. What did Paul value more than his own life?

B. Why do you think Paul compared his life to a race? What point was he trying to make? How does this point relate to you?

7. Read Colossians 1:21–23 and 3:23–24.

A. How is Colossians 1:21–23 an encouragement to finish strong? Why was "finishing strong" important to the apostle?

B. What command does Colossians 3:23 give us? What encouragement to obey this command are we given in 3:24? Does this help you to finish strong? Why or why not?

8. Steve writes, "It's *endurance* that separates the men from the boys. It's *endurance* that determines whether or not a man will finish strong. And *endurance* is the fruit of godly character."

A. Why do you think endurance is so critical to finishing strong?

B. On a scale of 1 (low) to 10 (high), rate your own endurance in the following categories:

Physical _____

Spiritual ____

Work ____

Marriage ____

Family ____

C. Are you satisfied with the ratings you gave yourself above? Why or why not? In the categories that give you the most dissatisfaction, what can you do to increase your endurance?

9. Steve writes, "It's never too late to begin doing what's right."
   A. Are you ever tempted to give up because of personal failure? In those times, how do you react to a statement like Steve's?
   B. Be honest: Are there any areas in your life right now in which you believe you have not been doing the right thing? Should the Holy Spirit bring any of these areas to mind, what do you plan to do about them?

10. Comment on the following line taken from an anonymous poem: "All you have to do to win—is rise each time you fall."
   A. Do you agree with this? Why or why not?
   B. When you fall, what makes it hard for you to rise? How do you overcome this obstacle?

11. Steve writes, "We don't finish strong by focusing on the finish line because we don't know where the finish line is. We finish strong by fixing our eyes on Jesus."
   A. What does it mean in practical terms to "fix your eyes on Jesus"? What does this entail? How do you know if you're doing it successfully or not?
   B. In what areas of life is it easiest for you to "fix your eyes on Jesus"? In what areas is it hardest?
   C. How would you help a new Christian "fix his eyes on Jesus"?

12. Steve says that ten of the twelve spies sent into the Promised Land failed because they "had a greater fear of man than they did of God."
   A. What does it mean to "fear God"?
   B. How can you tell if someone fears God?
   C. How can you tell if someone doesn't fear God (see Romans 3:10–18).
   D. How can you develop and nurture a healthy fear of God? Are you doing this? Explain.

13. Answer the following questions taken from this chapter:
   A. What makes you think that you will be the one man out of ten who will finish strong?
   B. What *exceptional measures* are you taking in your life to ensure that you will be the one out of ten?

CHAPTER TWO

FINISHING SO-SO

1. Steve describes four kinds of finishes and gives several biblical examples of each one. Do a brief study of each of the four categories by looking up each person mentioned. Then summarize what the people in each category have in common.

   A. Cut off early: Samson, Absalom, Josiah, John the Baptist, James

   B. Finished poorly: Gideon, Eli, Saul, Solomon

   C. Finished "so-so": David, Jehoshaphat, Hezekiah

   D. Finished well: Abraham, Joseph, Joshua, Caleb, Daniel, Paul, Peter

After you have done this, try to think of examples from your own life experience of people in each category. Finally, ask yourself a question: If I were to die tonight, into which category would I most likely fit? Why?

2. Steve writes, "The bottom line in determining how a man will finish centers around getting through the ambushes. To finish strong means that you survived the ambushes. Getting through the ambushes is what separates the men from the boys. And the guys who get through the ambushes are generally the guys who *anticipate the ambushes.*"

   A. How is it possible to "anticipate the ambushes"? Are you doing so? Explain.

   B. The first of the three major ambushes Steve talks about is "another woman." He cites several studies designed to probe into why men fall into adultery and lists several reasons for their fall, including:

      1. Lack of involvement in a personal accountability group
      2. Failure to have a daily time of prayer, Scripture reading, and worship
      3. Involved with unwise counseling situations
      4. Belief that moral failure could never happen to them

   Which of the four reasons above is (are) most likely to give you trouble? What do you intend to do about this?

   C. The second major ambush Steve lists is "money". He quotes Henry Fielding who said, "If you make money your god, it will plague you like the devil."

      1. In what way is money a major ambush?
      2. How is it possible to "make money your god"?
      3. How are you preparing for the ambush of money? How would you

characterize your attitude toward money? Would your friends and family agree with your assessment? Explain.

    D. The third major ambush Steve mentions is a "neglected family".

        1. Answer Steve's revised Bible quotation: "What shall it profit a man if he should win the whole world and lose his own family?"

        2. What is most likely to take you away from your own family? How do you deal with this?

        3. Try an experiment. Set some time aside this week to find out how your family thinks you're doing on this "ambush." Take half an hour with your wife and another half an hour for each of your kids to get their assessment. You could start by asking simple questions: "Am I spending enough time with you?" "Are we doing the things together that you really want to do?" "If we took a day off together, what would you want us to do?" Remember, this is a time to get their input. Just listen; don't defend yourself if you get the urge. Simply try to get their honest opinion about how you're doing with this third "ambush."

3. Read Acts 4:32–5:11.

    A. What was the "root sin" that led to the demise of Ananias and Sapphira? Was it lying? Greed? Hypocrisy? Explain your answer.

    B. What were the consequences of their sin?

    C. Why did "great fear" seize the whole church after this incident? What did the church learn about God?

    D. Does this knowledge still affect the church today? Does it affect you? Explain.

4. Steve writes, "The qualification for having a public ministry is not *giftedness*. The qualification for ministry is *proven character.*"

    A. In what way is proven character more important than giftedness in ministry?

    B. What do you tend to focus on, giftedness or proven character? Explain.

    C. Do you think you spend more time trying to hone your gifts, or build up your character? What specific things do you do to address each area?

5. Read 1 Timothy 3:4–5; 5:8.

    A. What qualifications does 1 Timothy 3:4–5 list for men being considered for church leadership? What does this mean? Why is it important? What does it show about the men?

B. In what ways can men fail to "provide for their families" (1 Timothy 5:8)? How would an unbeliever be better off? Why is this failure considered a denial of the faith?

6. Why should your answer to Steve's question, "Are you absolutely sure that you will finish strong?" be NO?

CHAPTER THREE

STAYING THE COURSE

1. Steve writes, "It's an appropriate exercise for a man who finds himself at middle age to evaluate how he's doing, now that he's reached the halfway point of the journey."

    A. Take some time to evaluate how you're doing in several important areas of life. Using a scale of 1 (poor) to 10 (excellent), rate yourself in each of the following categories:

        1. Marriage

        2. Family

        3. Spiritual life

        4. Work life

        5. Social life

        6. Recreational life

        7. Intellectual life

    B. Are you satisfied with the ratings you gave yourself? Why or why not? What area(s) need the most improvement? How could this midcourse correction be made?

2. Read Philippians 3:10–14.

    A. What five things did Paul want, according to verses 10–11? Do you also want these things? Explain.

    B. What was Paul's attitude as reflected in verses 12–13? Do you share such an attitude? Explain.

    C. What was Paul's "one thing"? How does this relate to finishing strong?

    D. What "prize" are you aiming for? Do you think you will get it? Why or why not?

3. Steve writes, "Not only is it good to evaluate the years you've already lived, but it's very wise to consider how you want to spend the rest of your life."

    A. How do you want to spend the rest of your life? What do you want to be doing in ten years? Twenty years? Thirty years? Beyond that?

    B. Consider the seven areas of life listed in question 1A above. What can you do now to raise the ratings you gave yourself? What would you have to do in the next ten years? Twenty years? Thirty years? Beyond that?

4. Reread Rolfe Kerr's mission statement as it is reproduced on page 46.
   A. Which of the 12 items listed would you like to adopt for your own mission statement? Explain.
   B. What do you like about this mission statement? What might you not like? Why?
   C. Do you have a personal mission statement? If so, what is it? If not, why not?

5. Steve's personal mission statement is "Don't screw up."
   A. What do you think of this? What do you like about it? What might you dislike?
   B. Whether or not you already have a personal mission statement, try now to develop a "short" mission statement in one sentence. How does this single sentence spell out for you what is most important to you?

6. Discuss the maxim, "If we leave the devil with even one small peg in our life, he will return to hang his rotting garbage on it."
   A. What "small peg" might the devil still own in your life? What will you do about it?
   B. Ask your best friend what "small peg" he thinks the devil might still own in your life. How does his evaluation compare with yours? How do you respond to his evaluation?

7. Consider each of Thomas Watson's "twenty-four nails." He said a godly man is a man:
   1. of knowledge
   2. moved by faith
   3. fired by love
   4. like God
   5. careful about the worship of God
   6. who serves God, not men
   7. who prizes Christ
   8. who weeps
   9. who loves the Word
   10. who has the Spirit of God residing in him
   11. who is humble
   12. who prays
   13. who is sincere

14. of heaven

15. of zeal

16. of patience

17. who gives thanks

18. who loves the saints

19. who does not indulge himself in any sin

20. who is good in his relationships

21. who does spiritual things in a spiritual manner

22. who is thoroughly trained in religion

23. who walks with God

24. who strives to help others grow in godliness

A. Again on a scale of 1 (poor) to 10 (excellent), rate yourself on each of these twenty-four "nails." Which are encouraging to you? Which give you concern? Why?

B. Do you agree with Watson that a man who embodies these qualities "is as sure to go to heaven as if he were in heaven already"? Why or why not?

8. Steve writes, "Guys who finish strong are stayed upon Jehovah."

A. What does it mean to be "stayed upon Jehovah"?

B. Are you "stayed upon Jehovah"? Explain

C. What, specifically, can a man do to become "stayed upon Jehovah"? Which of these things do you regularly do? Which do you struggle with? Explain.

9. Steve writes that if we want to finish strong, we need at least four "stays" to keep our integrity intact:

A. Stay in the Scriptures.

1. Read Joshua 1:8–9.

a. What did Joshua do to stay in the Scriptures? What can we do to follow his example?

2. Read Psalms119:11.

a. What did the psalmist do to stay in the Scriptures? How can we follow his example?

3. Steve suggests that we highlight a few verses that are especially meaningful or helpful to us, then write them on 3x5 cards or sticky notes and review them often throughout the day.

a. Pick one verse a week for the next month that you want to meditate upon. Write the four references here:

_____

_____

_____

_____

B. Stay close to a friend you can't con.
 1. Read Hebrews 3:12–13.
  a. What connection do you see between verses 12 and 13?
  b. Why does verse 13 depend on having friends you can't con?
 2. Read 2 Corinthians 1:3–5.
  a. How are we to respond when God comforts us?
  b. How do these verses show the necessity of having believing friends?
 3. Steve quotes Samuel Johnson as saying, "If a man does not make new acquaintances as he advances through life, he will soon find himself alone. A man, sir, must keep his friendships in constant repair."
  a. Are you making new acquaintances as you "advance through life"? Explain.
  b. What are you doing, specifically, to keep your friendships "in constant repair"?
C. Stay away from other women.
 1. Read 1 Thessalonians 4:3–8.
  a. What commands are given in verses 3–4?
  b. What contrast is described in verse 5?
  c. What command is given in verse 6? What warning?
  d. What general principle is laid out in verse 7?
  e. What conclusion is made in verse 8?
 2. Steve writes of "a 'theologically conservative' group of Christians whose behavior has absolutely no relationship to their doctrinal beliefs."
  a. From your own experience try to give an example of what Steve writes about.
  b. As you look at your own life, do you see any possible areas where your behavior seems to contradict your "theologically conservative" beliefs?
D. Stay alert to the tactics of the enemy.
 1. Read 1 Peter 5:8–9.

a. What are we told to do in verse 8? What reason for this is given?

b. What are we told to do in verse 9? What encouragement are we given to help us do this?

2. Steve quotes Martyn Lloyd-Jones as writing, "Not to realize that you are in a conflict means one thing only, and it is that you are so hopelessly defeated, and so 'knocked out' as it were, that you do not even know it—you are unconscious! It means that you are completely defeated by the devil."

a. How does "the conflict" most often appear in your experience? How do you respond to it?

b. Why would being unaware of the conflict mean that someone was already defeated?

10. Read Joshua 1:6–9.

A. What command was Joshua given in verse 6? What was the reason behind this command?

B. What additional command is given in verse 7? How does this relate to the previous command?

C. How is verse 8 an expansion of what was commanded in verse 7? What is the promised result for obedience?

D. What bedrock promise is given in verse 9? How does this promise encompass all of God's promises?

11. Read Hebrews 3:12–13.

A. What are we warned against in verse 12? How can you tell if someone has "a sinful, unbelieving heart that turns away from the living God"?

B. According to verse 13, how can we comply with the command of verse 12? Are you following this instruction? Explain.

12. Read 2 Peter 1:3–4.

A. What has God given us according to verse 3? What does this gift enable us to do?

B. What are we promised in verse 4? To whom is this promise given? To whom is it not given? What is the promised result? Are you experiencing what God promised here? Why or why not?

13. Steve encourages us, "Don't forget to spit." What does he mean? Are you

"spitting"? If so, what are you spitting? If not, why not?

14. Steve writes, "Have you ever given any thought to what you'd like to have inscribed on your grave marker?"

    A. Answer Steve's question. What would you like to have inscribed on your grave marker? Why?

CHAPTER FOUR

DRY SHIPWRECK

1. Steve writes, "That great leader of the next generation may be running around your house right now with a diaper that needs changing and a nose that needs wiping. So make sure you take good care of the kid."

    A. Do you ever stop to think that God might choose one of your kids to become a great leader? If God should choose your kids to be great leaders in their own generation, how would their upbringing help them as leaders? How might it hurt them? What can you do about this?

    B. What kind of care are you giving your kids right now? Is it suitable for a future leader? Explain.

2. Read 1 Samuel 16:1–13.

    A. Did Samuel guess who God had in mind to lead Israel? Did Jesse? What does this reveal about purely human reasoning?

    B. Do you think this incident in any fashion changed the way Jesse reared his youngest son? Explain. Had you been Jesse, would it have changed your parenting approach? If so, how? If not, why not?

3. Take several minutes to brainstorm the following:

    A. In what ways can sin take you farther than you wanted to go? As much as you feel comfortable in discussing this, describe how this has been true in your own experience.

    B. In what ways can sin keep you longer than you wanted to stay? As much as you feel comfortable in discussing this, describe how this has been true in your own experience.

    C. In what ways can sin cost you more than you wanted to pay? As much as you feel comfortable in discussing this, describe how this has been true in your own experience.

4. Read 2 Samuel 11.

    A. In what way does this chapter represent the major watershed in David's life?

    B. In your own words, describe the stages David went through in committing this most famous of sins.

C. Do the stages you described in B above help you to understand how temptation and sin takes place in your own experience? If so, explain.

5. David obeyed only part of Deuteronomy 17:14–17. Read this text and then answer the following questions.
   A. Which parts of this text did David obey? Which part did he disobey?
   B. What did David's example teach his son Solomon?
   C. What does David's example teach us about following God's instructions? Why do you think we so often forget or ignore this lesson?

6. Steve writes, "David had planned on only a discreet evening of adultery, yet within weeks he was guilty of betrayal, murder, and a heinous cover-up. And that was a winding road he'd never planned to travel."
   A. How does this statement illustrate the three insights in question 3 above?
   B. Does your own experience echo the lesson expressed above? If so, how?

7. Steve writes, "Deception *never* covers disobedience. It just makes it worse. Count on it, your sin *will* find you out."
   A. Why can deception never cover disobedience?
   B. How does deception make disobedience worse?
   C. In what way can the belief that "your sin will find you out" keep you out of trouble? When was the last time you meditated on this truth? Recommendation: Write out this phrase on a 3x5 card and ponder its message this week.

8. Read 2 Samuel 12:1–4.
   A. How do you think it was possible for David to become so angry over the sin of the man Nathan described to him, yet be so accepting of his own sin? What finally shook David to reality?
   B. What were the consequences of David's sin? How did they reach far beyond his own life?
   C. Have you ever had a "Nathan" do for you what the prophet did for David? If so and you feel comfortable doing so, explain.
   D. What do you suppose would have happened to David had his sin never been exposed? Why do you think God waited a year to expose it?

9. Steve writes, "There are painful consequences that follow even our confessed sin. *That's why we want to avoid sin in the first place.*"

    A. If we truly confess and repent of our sin, why do you think God many
times still allows the consequences to occur? What do you think might
happen if consequences never occurred?

    B. Does a desire to avoid unpleasant consequences ever keep you from
sinning? Should it? Explain.

10. Steve quotes Max Lucado as writing, "Mark it down. Compromise *chills*
the soul."

    A. How does compromise "chill the soul"? What does it mean to "chill the
soul"?

    B. What's the spiritual temperature of your own heart? Would your wife
and your best friend agree? Explain.

CHAPTER FIVE

THE STATUS BROTHERS AND THEIR NOT-QUITE RIGHT FIRST COUSIN, PRIDE

1. Steve quotes John Johnson, who wrote, "Success is attaining cultural goals that are sure to elevate one's perceived importance in that culture."

   A. Restate this observation in your own words.

   B. Steve lists three areas which are central to attaining "perceived impor-tance" in a culture. They are:
   * Power
   * Privilege
   * Wealth

   How do each of these contribute to someone's "perceived importance"? How eager are you to acquire each of them? Which presents you with the biggest temptation?

2. Read 2 Chronicles 26, paying special attention to verses 15 and 16.

   A. List the accomplishments of Uzziah's reign as described in this passage.

   B. Why is verse 15 a "hinge verse"?

   C. How did Uzziah respond when challenged in the temple? What does this show you about his heart?

   D. How did God respond to Uzziah's insolence?

   E. What lessons most speak to you from this passage? Why?

3. Steve writes, "Unless I miss my guess, I'd say the number one reason Uzziah ran into that terrible 'until' was that *he began to spend more time and attention on the external rather than the eternal.*"

   A. Why do you think this error is so common?

   B. How can a man tell if he's spending more time and attention on the external than the eternal? What evidence indicates this?

   C. Are you happy with the balance of time you spend on the external vs. internal? Explain.

4. Steve says that a second reason for Uzziah's tragic fall was that his char-acter did not keep pace with his accomplishments.

A. How did Uzziah's accomplishment outstrip his character?

B. What practical steps can we take to avoid the king's error? List as many as you can think of.

5. Steve writes, "One of the things about raising children is that you cannot impart that which you do not possess...character isn't something you mandate, it's something you model."

A. Do you agree that "you cannot impart that which you do not possess"? Explain.

B. What kind of character are you modeling for your kids? Rate yourself in each of the following areas, from 1 (poor) to 10 (excellent).
* Use of time _____
* Following through on commitments _____
* Treatment of others _____
* Use of money _____
* Recreational choices _____
* Honesty _____
* Healthy speech _____

C. Does your self-rating above suggest anything to you about any areas in which you need work? If so, what do you plan to do?

6. How did Uzziah's own success trip him up? How can the same thing happen to us? How can we avoid this trap?

7. Steve quotes Warren Wiersbe, who wrote, "If God puts something in my hand without first doing something to my heart, my character will lag behind my achievements, and that is the way to ruin."

A. What does Wiersbe mean? Do you agree with him? Explain.

B. What part do we play in ensuring that our character does not lag behind our achievements? What do you do regarding this important issue?

8. Read Proverbs 16:18.

A. How could heeding this verse have kept Uzziah from his tragic fall?

B. How can heeding this verse keep us from following Uzziah's example?

9. Steve writes, "At some point in his life, Uzziah gradually began to shift his trust from God to his accomplishments."

A. How can you tell if someone has shifted his trust from God to his accomplishments? What evidence is there of this shift?

   B. If a man has realized he is making (or is about to make) Uzziah's mistake, what can he do to correct it? What specific steps can he take?

   C. In what areas of your own life are you most likely to shift your trust from God to your accomplishments? What can you do to make sure this doesn't happen?

10. Steve writes, "Pride is like a degenerative eye disease that gradually blinds you. But its progress is so slow you don't even realize you're losing your spiritual vision—until it's too late."

   A. Without looking at a dictionary, how would you define pride?

   B. Steve lists two primary symptoms of pride: Arrogance and an aversion to accountability. Do you suffer from either of these two symptoms? If so, what does this suggest to you? What will you do about it?

11. Read 1 Samuel 16:7.

   A. How does this verse show that external accomplishments or appearances can be false indicators of success?

   B. How can you apply the truth of this verse to your work? At home? In church? In your neighborhood?

12. Read Romans 12:11.

   A. What is the connection in this verse between "zeal" (or "spiritual fervor") and "serving the Lord"? Which comes first? Explain.

   B. How does this truth help us to combat spiritual indifference and avoid Uzziah's error?

13. If we desire to combat spiritual indifference, we might do well to ask ourselves the following questions:

   * Am I seeking Jesus Christ the way I once did?

   * Am I hungrily diving into the Word the way I once did?

   * Am I enjoying the company of other believers as I once did?

   * Do I delight in quiet walks and talks with God the way I once did?

Ask yourself each of these questions, and remember, "It's not too late to move back into the sunlight! It's not too late to turn away from false standards of 'success' and seek the Lord with all your heart."

CHAPTER SIX

UNTEACHABLE,
UNACCOUNTABLE, AND
UNACCEPTABLE

1. Howard Hendricks defines a leader as "someone who leads."
   A. In what way is this definition wiser than it first appears?
   B. How can you tell if someone is leading others? What characterizes them? What doesn't characterize them?
   C. In what spheres of life are you a leader? Are you truly leading in these spheres? Explain.

2. Read 3 John 9–10.
   A. Why is it significant that the first trait John lists about Diotrephes is that he "loves to be first"? How does this automatically disqualify someone from biblical leadership?
   B. Why do you think Diotrephes would "have nothing to do with" John? What does this tell you about the man?
   C. Why do many people who usurp positions of authority "gossip maliciously" about others in authority? What do they hope to accomplish?
   D. Why is hospitality so important for a leader? Was Diotrephes hospitable? How do you know?
   E. Do any of the traits of Diotrephes also characterize your life? Be honest about this. If so, what can you do about it *today*?

3. Read 1 Peter 5:1–4.
   A. What positive characteristics of a godly leader does Peter list in this passage?
   B. What does he tell leaders to avoid?
   C. What promise does he give?
   D. How do you stack up against Peter's description of a godly leader? Where are you strongest? Weakest?

4. Steve lists five characteristics of an UnLeader. They include:
   A. An UnLeader is an UnServant.

1. Read Mark 9:35; Matthew 20:26–8.

a. What do you learn about leadership from these verses?

b. How do you put these verses into practice in the way that you lead?

c. Steve says that "Christian leadership is giving your best without having to be first." Describe the leader in your own experience who best lived out this definition. What have you learned from this person?

B. An UnLeader is UnTeachable.

1. Steve writes, "Let's put it on the table. If you're not teachable, you don't have a chance in the world of finishing strong. Not a chance."

a. Why do you think Steve makes such a strong, unqualified statement? Do you agree with him? Explain.

b. How "teachable" are you? Describe any areas in which it is particularly difficult for you to be teachable. What makes these areas so difficult? How can you address them positively?

C. An UnLeader is UnJust.

1. Steve writes, "Words are awesomely powerful instruments—for evil or good. And in a Christian home, there is no room for unjust words."

a. Think back to your own growing up years. What "unjust words" were spoken there? What effect did they have on you?

b. Fast forward to your own home. In the past week, what "unjust words" were spoken there? What effect did they have on members of your family? Were you responsible for any of these unjust words?

c. Write down any "unjust words" that you have a tendency to say in the following left-hand column; then in the right-hand column replace them with "just" words, words that would help rather than harm.

Unjust	Just

D. An UnLeader is UnHospitable.

1. Steve writes, "Hospitality...isn't always convenient. It isn't always comfortable and handy. It doesn't always fit right in with our plans and our schedules."

a. How often in an average month do you extend hospitality to someone? How do you do this?

b. What aspects of hospitality do you find most difficult? What kind of hospitality is most uncomfortable for you? Why?

c. Giving hospitality involves more than just you; your wife is a big part of it. Take some time to talk over this issue with her. How does she feel about it? Would she like to do more or less of it? Why? How can you work together to be hospitable people?

E. An UnLeader has an UnHappy family.

1. Do you consider your family a "happy" group? Explain.

2. What makes your family happy? Unhappy? Does any of this have to deal with your leadership style? Explain.

3. Steve writes, "We can have false gods in our lives, too. We can be nourished by gods other than the true and living God."

a. What kinds of "false gods" do people in your acquaintance have? Describe them.

b. What kinds of "false gods" are you most susceptible to? How can you deal with them?

CHAPTER SEVEN

LOUSY START, STRONG FINISH

1. Read 2 Kings 21:1–17 and 2 Chronicles 33:1–20.

   A. List the evils Manasseh committed that are mentioned in these passages.

   B. How did God respond to Manasseh's evil?

   C. How did Manasseh respond to God's discipline?

   D. How did God respond to Manasseh's change of heart?

   E. What does this story teach us about sin and repentance? Do you think Manasseh should have been forgiven? Explain.

   F. In what ways do you see yourself as similar to Manasseh? In what ways are you different?

2. Steve writes, "Whenever you and I deviate from God's best for us, He speaks to our hearts. He usually speaks quietly at first, in that distinctive 'still, small voice.'"

   A. How does God normally speak to you when you "deviate from God's best"? How do you usually respond?

   B. How can we better attune our ears to hear God's "still, small voice"? What practical steps can we take to become more sensitive to His voice?

3. Steve writes, "If we continue in our sin, [God] will often put some people around us who will carefully and lovingly challenge us about our sin."

   A. Do you have anyone in your life who "carefully and lovingly" challenges you about your sin? If so, describe the person. If not, why not?

4. Steve writes, "In case you haven't noticed by now, God isn't like you and me. He is radically different from what we are like."

   A. In what ways is God different from us?

   B. Are there any ways in which God is similar to us? (Think of the phrase, "made in the image of God".)

   C. Are you glad that "God is radically different from what we are like"? Explain.

5. Steve writes, "This human heart of mine is just as corrupt as [Manasseh's]

...and so is yours. Maybe we haven't sinned to the same degree, but trust me on this...we're made of the exact same stuff. And don't kid yourself; except for the grace of God, we have the potential to do precisely what he did."

    A. Do you believe your own heart is as corrupt as was Manasseh's? Why or why not?

    B. Why do you think Steve places such emphasis on this point? What does this have to do with finishing strong?

6. Steve writes that "Genuine repentance...unlocks the floodgates of God's amazing mercy."

    A. How can repentance be phony? Do you ever catch yourself doing "phony repentance"? How do you recognize it?

    B. How does genuine repentance unlock the floodgates of God's mercy? How does this principle operate in your own life?

7. Steve writes, "Genuine repentance always brings evidence with it. That's how you recognize it."

    A. What kind of "evidence" do you think Steve means? How do you recognize genuine repentance?

    B. Read Acts 26:20.

       1. What does Paul say he preached to everyone he met? What kind of "deeds" do you think he was talking about?

    C. Read Titus 1:16.

       1. What "claim" do many people make, according to Paul?

       2. How is this claim proven false?

       3. How does Paul characterize those who falsely make this claim?

8. Read 1 Corinthians 6:9–11.

    A. By what are some people "deceived," according to this passage?

    B. What is Paul's point in listing the various types of sin mentioned in this passage? What is he trying to get the Corinthians to see?

    C. What major contrast does Paul make in verse 11? What does Paul now assume about the lifestyles of these people?

9. Steve says that ignorance of Bible teaching can chain us to the past.

    A. Read John 19:30. To what was Jesus referring when he said, "It is finished"? How are His words a powerful tonic for a wounded soul?

B. Read Hebrews 10:10–18. How does this passage make clear what Jesus meant when He said, "It is finished"? How does it free us from guilt and shame?

C. Read Psalms 103:10–12. According to what principle has God *not* treated us? According to what principle has God treated us? Why should we be eternally grateful for this?

D. How extensive is your own knowledge of Bible teaching? How are you working to increase it?

10. Steve writes that unbelief can also chain us to the past.

A. Read Luke 24:25. Of what sin does Jesus accuse His disciples in this verse? How had their sin hurt them?

B. Read 1 John 1:9. What promise is made here? How would failure to believe this promise chain you to the past?

C. Are there any areas of "unbelief" which hamper your own spiritual life? If so, what are they? Describe them. How have you addressed these areas in the past? How do you think you can more effectively address them in the future?

11. Steve writes that "My past life does not exclude me from present service."

A. What reasons does he give for saying this? Do you believe him? Why or why not?

B. What difference does this make to you?

C. In what areas are you currently serving the Lord? Are you satisfied with your record of service? Explain.

12. Steve writes, "I don't care who you are, or what you have done, or how evil you have been. If God could forgive Manasseh, He can forgive you."

A. Have you ever felt that what you had done was too wicked to forgive? If so, explain. How did you overcome this feeling?

B. Take some extended time to thank God that He has forgiven you of all your sins, whatever they have been, because of your faith in what Jesus did for you on the cross.

CHAPTER EIGHT

FAILURE THAT EQUIPS YOU TO FINISH

1. Steve writes, "As Moses contemplated going to the aid of his Hebrew brother, Scripture says that 'he looked this way and that.' In other words, he looked around to his left and then to his right. But do you know what he failed to do? He never looked *up*."

    A. What's so important about looking up? How might Moses' story have been different had he looked up?

    B. How might your own story be different had you consistently looked up in the past?

    C. Are you looking up now? Explain.

2. Steve says that what makes the difference between healthy self-confidence or self-esteem and excessive self-confidence is prayerlessness.

    A. What do you think he means? Do you agree with him? Why or why not?

    B. How much time do you think you spend in prayer each week? Each day? Are you satisfied with this amount of time? Explain.

    C. The best way to increase the amount of time you spend talking with God is NOT to try to add large time blocks, but to increase your prayer times in small increments. Try something like the following suggestions:

        1. If you're not praying at all, try to spend five minutes every other day talking to God; after a month, expand it to five minutes every day.

        2. If you're praying sporadically, try to set a regular time and place to pray—say, for ten minutes five times a week.

        3. If your prayer life is pretty regular but you'd like to expand it further, try praying through the Psalms. Or do a study on the prayers of the Bible and follow the examples you see there. Or concentrate on a different type of prayer on the various days of the week: for example, use Monday for special praises, Tuesday for intercession for others, Wednesday for requests for your family, etc.

3. Steve lists four core classes in Moses' "master's education." They are:

    A. Unemployment 101

        1. Steve says this course is so hard because it:

* attacks a man's self-worth
* lasts an indefinite time

a. Have you ever had to take "Unemployment 101"? If so, describe your experience. Did it attack your self-worth? How long did it last—or are you still enrolled?

b. How did you make it through (or how will you make it through) this course?

c. What advice would you give to others enrolled in this course?

B. Advanced Obscurity

1. Steve writes, "There is one tried and tested remedy for overconfidence. It is obscurity."

a. Why is obscurity such a good cure for overconfidence? How does it "cure" it?

b. Has God ever used "Advanced Obscurity" to deal with your own overconfidence? If so, describe what happened.

2. Steve writes, "God always has a deeper purpose when He puts His people in this course of Advanced Obscurity."

a. If you have gone through Advanced Obscurity, do you know what purpose it was to serve? If so, describe it.

b. If you are enrolled in Advanced Obscurity right now, what purpose do you think it might be intended to serve?

c. How does it help to know that God has not forgotten us, even if we are stuck in Advanced Obscurity?

C. Remedial Waiting

1. Steve writes, "I've got some bad news for you. You may be in a hurry, but God is not in a hurry."

a. Why do you think God is so seldom in a hurry?

b. How does it make you feel that waiting is one of God's favorite tools for shaping our character?

c. What kind of Remedial Waiting are you doing right now? What kind of Remedial Waiting has God enrolled you in before? What did it accomplish *in you?*

2. Steve writes, "[God] knows *precisely* what He is doing in your life. Every trial has a beginning, a middle, and an end. You cannot determine where you are in your trial, but He knows exactly where you are. And He is moving you along at just the right pace."

a. Does it help to know that God is in absolute control of your circumstances? Why or why not?

b. How do you normally respond to God when He has you in a holding pattern?

c. For an interesting further study, get an exhaustive concordance and look up the many references to "wait," "waiting" and "waited" in the Scriptures. What do you learn?

D. Intermediate Loneliness

1. Steve writes, "A leader really isn't a leader until he has learned to follow."

a. Why can't a leader be a good leader without learning first to follow?

b. What kind of a follower are you? Describe some of the leaders whom you follow.

2. Steve writes, "Loneliness is never a pleasant experience. But God, in His wisdom, at times will separate us from our normal network of family and friends. Isolation is an opportunity to get to know Him better.

a. How do you deal with loneliness when it comes?

b. Have you ever thought of loneliness as a tool to make you more resemble Jesus? Explain.

c. What might God be desiring to teach you right now through loneliness?

4. Read John 15:1–8.

A. What does it mean to "abide" or "remain" in Jesus?

B. To what does Jesus compare Himself in verse 5? To what does He compare His disciples? What is His point?

C. What happens to a man who "remains in" Jesus? What is the result? What is meant by the term "fruit"? What kind of "fruit" are you bearing?

D. What does Jesus mean when He says, "Apart from me you can do nothing"? How literally should this be taken? Explain. How do we often show that we don't believe Him?

E. Are you bearing "much fruit," as Jesus describes in verse 8? Explain. If not, what is the cause? What remedy does Jesus give?

5. Read Philippians 3:13–14.

A. What failures did Paul leave behind him? What successes?

B. How is this text a perfect one for someone who is failing? In what way does it apply to all of us, regardless of our circumstances?

6. Steve writes, "When you look behind the scenes at some of the most successful people in all of history, you will find that they were not unacquainted with failure. And it was failure that became the bedrock that enabled them to handle the triumphs that came later."

    A. How does failure help us to handle later triumphs?

    B. What failures may God be using in your own life right now? How are you handling these failures?

7. Steve writes, "The people God loves to use most are those who have learned to depend completely upon Him. For many of us self-sufficient, confident types, that doesn't come easily."

    A. What does it mean to "depend completely upon Him"? Does this mean we sit back and do nothing, waiting for God to act? Explain.

    B. How easy is it for you to depend upon God? How do you express your dependence? How do others recognize it?

CHAPTER NINE

156 BUCK-NAKED MILES TO BIGHORN

1. Steve writes, "Are you worried that you don't have much of a network? Joseph didn't either. But he had a Friend in High Places. And if you have surrendered your life to Christ, so do you. It's all the network you'll ever need."

    A. Have you surrendered your life to Christ? If so, describe how this came about. If not, why not?

    B. Why is a "Friend in High Places" all the network you'll ever need? Do you utilize this network? Explain.

2. Steve writes, "The man who finishes so-so has kept back one or two areas of his life from the Lord. His theme song is 'I Surrender Ninety-Five Percent.'"

    A. Are you on track to finish strong...or just so-so? How can you tell?

    B. What five percent are you most unwilling to surrender to the Lord? Why?

3. According to Genesis 39:7–20, Joseph put away the thought of trading his purity for his position.

    A. How did he do this? What kept him from this sin?

    B. How can Joseph be a model for us in similar circumstances?

4. According to Genesis 50:15–21, Joseph put away the thought of turning his betrayal into bitterness.

    A. What prompted him to do this?

    B. How can we follow Joseph's example?

5. Read 1 Corinthians 2:9.

    A. How can this verse be a powerful encouragement for us to finish strong? What promise does it make?

6. Read Ephesians 4:30–32.

    A. What are we instructed to refrain from doing in verse 30? What reason is given for refraining from this? How can this reason be a powerful motivator for finishing strong?

    B. What are we told to avoid in verse 31? Which of these do you most

struggle with? How can you begin to comply with this command?
C. What are we told to do in verse 32? What reason are we given for doing so?

7. Steve says that in all of our lives there are things that God will take away as well as things which we must put away.
   A. What have been some of the things in your life that God has taken away? Why do you think He did this?
   B. What are some of the things that you believe you must put away? Why these things? When do you plan on putting them away? How will you do this?

8. Steve writes, "God is able to take the hateful and hurtful motivation of your enemies and use them to accomplish His plan in your life. These things won't keep you from God's best...they will help you to reach God's best. For it is in the deep and dark experiences of betrayal, when we wrestle with the giant of bitterness, that we begin to build spiritual muscle."
   A. How has God used the "hateful and hurtful motivations of your enemies" in your life to accomplish His plan?
   B. How can God use even betrayal to help you finish strong?
   C. Are you wrestling with the giant of bitterness right now? If so, who's winning? How can you make sure the right side ends up the victor?

9. Read Hebrews 12:15.
   A. How is it possible to "miss the grace of God"?
   B. Why do you think the writer uses the image of a growing root to speak of bitterness? What is especially appropriate about this image?
   C. What two things does unchecked bitterness do, according to this verse?

10. Steve writes, "Take the lance of the Word of God and drive it through the very heart of that pursuing bitterness. Pin that thing to the ground. And get on with the race. The sooner you get on with it, the sooner you will discover the blessings that God has for you."
   A. How can you use God's Word to pierce the "very heart" of a persistent bitterness?

B. What blessings has God already shown to you and bestowed upon you? Does this prompt you to desire to continue the race? Explain.

CHAPTER TEN

A VISION FOR THE FINISH LINE

1. Steve writes, "What's the big deal about vision? Some people have it, some don't. The big deal about vision is this. It takes vision to finish strong."
   A. Why does it take vision to finish strong?
   B. What is the vision you have that will help you finish strong?

2. Steve asks three questions you should answer:
   A. What do you want your life to look like in ten years?
   B. How about twenty years?
   C. What do you want your children's lives to look like in ten years?

3. Steve writes, "In order to finish strong, we must have vision. Vision for what is really important, vision for what our kids really need, and the vision to steel ourselves against the strategies of the enemy to destroy everything near and dear to our hearts."
   A. Describe your own vision in each of these areas:
     * Vision for what is really important
     * Vision for what our kids really need
     * Vision to steel ourselves against the strategies of the enemy
   B. How will each of these visions help you to finish strong?

4. Steve says that guys in various decades of life should have visions appropriate to their age, yet they don't always.
   A. Guys in their twenties and thirties should have "vision to look forty years into the future and think about how they want to finish."
     1. If you are at this stage, how do you see yourself finishing? What strategies will it take to get you there?
     2. If you are past this stage, what did you envision at this stage? Are you on track? Explain.
   B. Guys in their forties and fifties sometimes "get sloppy spiritually and put it on cruise control."
     1. If you have yet to reach this age, how will you prevent the trouble Steve warns against?

2. If you are at this stage, how are you combating this tendency? How are you doing?

3. If you are past this stage, how did you do? Were you able to overcome this tendency? If so, how did you do it? If not, what tripped you up?

C. Guys in their sixties and seventies "realize that little grandchildren are the leaders of a future generation. It takes vision to spend time with them instead of cruising the country six months out of the year in a Winnebago."

1. If you have yet to reach this stage, how are you preparing now to minister to your own grandkids?

2. If you are at this stage, what are you doing to minister to your grandkids? What kind of spiritual example are you setting for them?

5. Steve writes, "Here we are, two thousand years [after the resurrection of Christ]. And isn't it interesting that we name our children Peter and Paul, Mary and Martha? And we name our dogs Caesar and Nero."

A. How does this observation help us to keep our eyes on the eternal?

B. Who are the modern-day Caesars and Neros? Why is it so easy to get sidetracked by their antics?

C. What one thought from this book has most helped you to finish strong?

D. Is there anything in your life right now that, if left unchecked, would keep you from finishing strong? If so, how do you plan to deal with it?

E. Spend some time alone with your Heavenly Father, thanking Him that it is only through the power of His Spirit that any of us finish strong. Ask Him to keep you on track, to depend upon His strength and wisdom and not your own. Praise Him for His goodness and thank Him for seeing you through the difficult times you've already experienced. And ask Him to enable you to look to His grace for the successful completion of the race He's set before you.